ASSHOLES

Also by James Felton

52 Times Britain was a Bellend

Sunburn

You Don't Want to Know

The Year was 2021

ASSHOLES

THE DEAD PEOPLE YOU SHOULD BE MAD AT

JAMES FELTON

SPHERE

SPHERE

First published in Great Britain in 2022 by Sphere

3 5 7 9 10 8 6 4 2

A CIP catalogue record for this book
is available from the British Library.

ISBN 978-0-7515-8582-7

Typeset in Caslon by M Rules
Printed and bound in Great Britain by Clays Ltd, Elcograf S.p.A.

Papers used by Sphere are from well-managed forests
and other responsible sources.

Sphere
An imprint of
Little, Brown Book Group
Carmelite House
50 Victoria Embankment
London EC4Y 0DZ

An Hachette UK Company
www.hachette.co.uk

www.littlebrown.co.uk

For Katie, Hugo and Dylan

INTRODUCTION

Assholes fascinate me. I would like to stress here that I mean people who are assholes, not the human exit. Anyone wanting to read a book about sphincters, I thoroughly recommend the David Cameron autobiography.

The great thing about history – for people interested in reading about terrible people from the past, not the people actually from the past getting Vlad the Impalered – is that it's not exactly short on cartoonishly evil bellends to read about. People who do the wrong thing – whether through malice, laziness or desperately trying to dig themselves out of a hole – will be discussed here and judged at length. Some are even heroic people who just happened to conduct their heroism in the manner befitting a dickhead.

Before we begin, a few caveats: I am primarily a comedy writer who has been given the opportunity to go back through history and dunk on the terrible people I happen across. The advantage of this is that I am not as jaded as historians who are so used to reading sentences like 'and then he did pour boiling acid onto his nephew, for he was bored' that they merely nod and say 'seems about right for the time' and move on. Be assured that the people discussed in this book were generally considered to be tools in their own day, but, equally, they won't be let off for being from an age where impaling your friends on a big spike or chopping off their genitals was just something you did to fill a quiet Tuesday.

Another advantage of me taking you through history's biggest assholes is that while historians may tell you the historical context in more detail, sometimes it's more fun to have a comedian tell you precisely in what way historical figures were gigantic cunts.

I will be focusing on people who you haven't heard of, rather than the jerks that you have, and have included some oddball assholes as well as some massive ones. I hope this will keep things more fun and fresh, and, honestly, if you need to learn precisely why Hitler was bad you probably need to learn it from a book serious enough not to have an anus on the cover. You'll also notice there are relatively few women included – not because I believe their asshole-ish antics aren't worthy of a mention, but because history seldom mentions their stories.

Now settle in as we take a look at the assholes of history, and the dead people you should be mad at.

DOMITIAN

Domitian became Roman emperor in 81 AD. It's difficult to stand out as an asshole only forty-eight years after another emperor executed Jesus, but Domitian gave it a try. On official state matters, he wasn't *too* bad, having finished the Colosseum, strengthened the economy, and, crucially, killed zero Jesuses.

However, the man had a cruel streak that was evident from day one. How evident, you ask? 'At the beginning of his reign he used to spend hours in seclusion every day,' Suetonius, the Roman historian and contemporary to Domitian, wrote, 'doing nothing but catch flies and stab them with a keenly-sharpened stylus.'[1]

OK, I'm not going to mourn a two-thousand-year-old fly, even if it did get brutally murdered by an emperor, but his sadism got worse from there. Like seemingly every other emperor who had ever held power, Domitian began to get paranoid that there were conspirators around him. In an attempt to get the names of these so-called conspirators out of his enemies, he allowed for a new type of interrogation: inserting fire into their genitals.[2] If there's one thing that gets you blurting out names of co-conspirators – real or not – it's a bonfire on the inside of your penis.

He also took an odd pleasure in treating people he was, unbeknownst to them, about to crucify. He would go as far as inviting them round for a chat and a dinner, very much giving them that 'not about to be executed' vibe you get from dinner with a friend, but then, unlike a friend, he would spoil things by executing the shit out of you.

Competing for space in quite a fucked-up personality chart was his hubris. Domitian liked to see his face everywhere, which was a pain given that the modern mirror wasn't invented until 1835.[3] Instead, he had so many gold and silver statues erected around Rome in his image that someone graffitied on one of them in Greek 'It is enough'.[4] This was nothing next to his insistence that people call him 'our Master and our God', and his decision to rename two months – September and October – after himself, becoming 'Germanicus' – his assumed surname – and 'Domitianus'. As tough as it was to live under Johnson, imagine getting to August and having to arrange to meet people the following month on 'the 30th of Boris'.

Domitian entertained senators and knights, according to contemporary historian Cassius Dio.[5] In another incidence of what can only be described as dinner shenanigans, Domitian first made sure that the entire party area was pitch black, before making guests come in without their usual entourage, or servants and slaves as they are more accurately known today. The guests, once they found their way to the table, were given a slab shaped like a gravestone. In case that was too subtle, the guests' names were inscribed on their personal tombstone. Again, this would be fine if you were a) not presented with this by a man known for executing people on a whim, and b) living in a time after the invention of Halloween. The guests, unable to tick off either of these two from their mental checklists, were then treated to a dance by boys who were naked, but painted entirely in black. The idea was that they would appear like phantoms, but, to be honest, once you've realised that your host has hired and painted naked boys to dance at you, you're probably terrified enough as it is and any guesses like 'Oh, are they also supposed to be ghosts?' are just window-dressing at that point. The only thing that broke the silence, in which the guests probably believed they could have their throats cut at any second, was Domitian talking 'only upon topics relating to death and slaughter'. He kept this up all evening, before sending them home by carriage, where they awaited death in the comfort of their own homes. He had given his guests lavish gifts, presented to them by the naked dancers from earlier, who had been 'washed and adorned'. Among these gifts were the gravestones, which turned out to be made of silver.

This, an evening of mortal peril followed by a thank-you gift, was Domitian attempting to be fucking *nice*.

Eventually, in 96 AD, Domitian was killed by a lower-class member of the imperial court. His undoing wasn't by one of the people he had been trying to locate via putting fire up people's pee-pee holes. He was killed by someone who feared for their own safety, and, let's face it, probably the safety of their pee-pee hole as well, following the recent execution of Domitian's former secretary and ally. Whether he could have found out about the potential plotter by setting fire to more pee-pee holes, or whether the assassin wouldn't have felt so unsafe had Domitian burned a few less pee-pee holes, we will never know. All we can say for certain is that Domitian didn't burn the exact right amount of pee-pee holes.

THE DOCTOR WHO LIKED TO MAKE BABIES CRY

For a long time, 'psychologist' meant 'someone who is willing to fuck with people for fun'. One such man worthy of the title was John B. Watson, who liked to make little children cry. You'll already be familiar with Pavlov's 1897 experiment in which the physiologist succeeded in showing that dogs could be conditioned to salivate whenever they heard a bell, if they had been made to associate it with food. Well, a couple of decades later, in 1919, Watson decided to conduct a similar experiment, asking the question, 'Can I do this but instead of dogs it'll be kids, and instead of food it'll be bunnies, and instead of salivation I'll make the kids shit themselves in fear?'

Watson acquired himself a baby, the son of a wet nurse at the hospital he was attached to. The boy, known as Little Albert, was described as 'stolid and unemotional' and as one who 'practically never cried'.[1] Albert, however, was about to learn about bastards.

Watson took Albert, who was eleven months old, and tested his responses to various stimuli to get a baseline measurement. He was shown a monkey, a rabbit, a rat and a dog, all of which he tried to play with, as well as fluffy bits of cotton and various hairy and non-hairy masks. In a groundbreaking bit of research, Watson's team then got a long steel rod and placed it behind Albert's head. They smacked the rod with a claw hammer, discovering that babies do not like terrifying sounds of claw hammers being struck behind their heads.

'The child started violently, his breathing was checked and the arms were raised in a characteristic manner,' Watson wrote,[2] before continuing with the process as if the fact that Albert hardly ever cried offended him. 'On the second stimulation the same thing occurred, and in addition the lips began to pucker and tremble. On the third stimulation the child broke into a sudden crying fit. This is the first time an emotional situation in the laboratory has produced any fear or even crying in Albert.'

The next step was to combine stimuli to see if they could transfer Albert's terrified reaction to the claw hammer striking metal onto a fluffy wickle doggy or bunny wabbit, and really make him shit himself if he ever came across the film *Zootropolis*. Small note, but if you're a psychiatrist, and one of your aims is to make a child piss himself when a bell goes ding, the only difference between you and a psychopath is a clipboard.

First the scientists took a white rat, and let the boy play with it for a time, which he gladly did. They then twatted the metal pole, startling Albert into falling over. He was again given the rat to play with, and the moment he touched it, the pole was struck again, making him fall over. This continued until the baby started crying his face off, which the psychologist took as a job well done. This just goes to show that sometimes it's difficult to distinguish between job descriptions of an early psychologist and the Child Catcher from *Chitty Chitty Bang Bang*. From then on, whenever a rat was presented to Albert, the baby would whimper, cry and 'crawl away so rapidly that he was caught with difficulty before reaching the edge of the table'.[3]

They then tested to see if this fear was just of rats, or if it also applied to other, fluffier animals. Albert was brought back in for some follow-ups, where he was presented with bunnies and other objects, while occasionally being given a refresher with the rat and the loud clanging sound to make sure it was still making him shit it. They also used the clanging sounds with dogs to see if it produced the same results.

The psychologist was elated. This kid was fucking terrified. He'd see a rabbit, he'd shit himself; he'd see a dog, he'd whimper in fear and shake violently; he'd see a psychologist wearing a fluffy Santa mask and would act like he'd just run into Leather Face from *The Texas Chain Saw Massacre*. For you, this would be a moment to look at yourself and ask 'What the hell have I become?', but for Watson it was champagne time.

Albert was taken away from the hospital on the day of the final tests, sort of suggesting that his mother had walked in on Watson leering at her crying child while in the Santa mask, and had made the excellent decision to flee, which unfortunately doesn't negate the fact that she gave her baby to a strange doctor grinning maniacally and holding a claw hammer in the first place.

The scientists had also planned to decondition Albert in the creepiest manner possible, 'by showing objects calling out fear responses (visual) and simultaneously stimulating the erogenous zones (tactual). We should try first the lips, then the nipples and as a final resort the sex organs.'[4] As if it would be better as an adult if he was shown a potential partner's dog, only for them to say, 'Would you like me to shut Cleo in the kitchen? It's just you're quite noticeably scared and, if I may say so, fully erect.'

EMPEROR QIN SHI HUANG

Before Emperor Qin Shi Huang, what is now China was a number of disparate states, some as different as Paris, France is from Paris, Texas – a place that ordered its own smaller Eiffel Tower and then genuinely topped it with a giant red cowboy hat. Each Chinese state even had their own calendars[1] and their writing was diverging, making it very difficult to write 'what the fuck do you mean it's Tuesday' in a way that someone from a different region would understand. Qin Shi Huang changed all that, uniting the states and becoming the first emperor of China in 221 BC. Whether you congratulate him, however, depends on whether you're on board with imperialism in general, as well as mass castrations and slavery specifically. Plus, of course, there was the time he buried four hundred people for the crime of not being as thick as he was.

On becoming king of the smaller region of Qin in 259 BC at just thirteen years old, Qin Shi Huang began his reign by executing his mother's lover (and his rival for the throne). He then imprisoned his mother and executed his half-siblings, which, apart from everything else, must have really fucked up Christmas. Qin Shi Huang then set about developing an army, and used it to aggressively grow his empire. As he went, he captured citizens and enslaved them, castrating them for good measure. Though proving himself as a man who'd clearly be better suited as a vet, he eventually took the whole of China by force, and became its sole leader. During his time as ruler, he attempted to standardise a lot of the things he'd found so annoying before, including writing, calendars, and axle length (to solve the situation of road sizes being wildly different, which had been causing problems at the time).

When he wasn't acting like a pedant ('Ooh actually I think you'll find the standardised axle length is this') or demanding the removal of people's testicles, Qin often spent his time being paranoid as hell – though it's easy to see why, given that he had thus far survived several assassination attempts, including one from a lute player.

The lute player had been in the middle of shredding a solo when it was pointed out to Qin that he was a friend of one of his enemies.[2] Rather than simply kill him (it's hard to get a tune out of worm food), Qin ordered that the lute player's eyes be gouged out, before allowing him to continue to rock on, or whatever the equivalent of that is in ancient China. However, the player's lute had been reinforced with lead, and after the gouging he swung it blindly at the emperor in an attempt to lute him to death, resulting in his being executed for attempting to kill the emperor.

Now, I realise that being able to play a musical instrument isn't necessarily an indication that you *aren't* a bloodthirsty assassin. However, you've got to ask yourself the question 'Maybe it's me?' when someone is attempting to kill you and what they're primarily known for is playing absolute bangers on what is essentially a medieval ukulele. Imagine being such a dickhead there's an assassination attempt on you by, e.g., a flautist.

After these assassination attempts, and out of paranoia, Qin would kill anyone who showed hints of opposing him. He also became convinced that poetry, history and philosophy were dangerous, as if his iron-fist rule was about to be overthrown by a particularly cutting limerick. (Maybe he thought that poets were the natural bedfellows of people who play the lute.) Naturally, he had books burned on a massive scale, and potentially (though evidence is far more dubious on this point[3]) buried over four hundred scholars alive. This latter act allegedly later inspired Chairman Mao Zedong, who bragged '[Qin] buried 460 scholars alive; we have buried 46,000 scholars alive.'[4] Despite all the other terrible things he did, Qin primarily makes the cut for this book for being so much of an asshole that he inspired Chairman Mao.

QUEEN RANAVALONA I

The system of having kings and queens is perfect. What better way to rule a country than simply crossing your fingers that the next infant to pop out of a queen's vagina happens to not be a horrific brutal dictator type? Throw in a little incest in order to maintain royal lines and a sense of entitlement from believing you've been put on the throne by God, and you have yourself a recipe for good governance. Just ask anyone who lived under Queen Ranavalona I of Madagascar whether the system is great and they'd have surely told you it was – and definitely not because they were living in fear of saying 'I have a few quibbles' and being force-fed their own testicles.

This story, of course, has two assholes: the Queen herself and anybody European. Ranavalona – quite understandably given that she reigned from 1828 to 1861, a time during which Africa was being colonised by several European powers – wasn't a fan of the French, or indeed other colonial powers. During her reign, she drew the Merina kingdom in Madagascar away from these colonial powers – often fighting them off effectively. She also attempted to make the nation self-sufficient (albeit through a system of the enforced slavery of anybody who was poor or looked at her funny). But in her reaction to colonial threats, and her desire to turn the clock back to a time before it all began, she brought back a number of practices that would result in many cruel and needless deaths of her subjects.

After the death of her husband, King Radama, in 1828, Ranavalona took over the island. By the time her reign had ended (by which I mean she was dead – what a great system!) in 1861, she had managed to halve the population to 2.5 million subjects, which, to be fair, probably helped with the self-sufficiency thing. Say what you will about the dead, but those lads are unlikely to demand any food.

Technically, it was Radama's nephew, Rakotobe, who should have taken over the throne according to the rules in place. However, Ranavalona was able to find a loophole in the law: Rakatobe can't rule if he and most of his family have been executed. After shoring up power, she had her nephew and his mother killed, as well as several other relatives, and became the first female ruler of Madagascar.

One of the stranger parts of her reign was the reintroduction of trial by eating chicken skins, were you to commit a crime. If you're picturing trials by combat, but with a big bucket of KFC, you aren't that far from the truth. Instead of trial by jury, Ranavalona would have the accused eat three chicken skins, as well as some poison made from the nuts of the tangena tree. The rule was that if you threw up all of the chicken skins you were innocent, but if you failed to puke up all three you were displaying the skinless chunder of the guilty. If you're thinking you could easily puke up three chicken skins, that's probably true and well done you. However, by 1839, the trials were estimated to have killed about a hundred thousand people due to the poisonings,[1] which was about 20 per cent of the population. So sort of exactly like KFC (please note for the lawyers' sake that this was a needless burn on KFC, which is actually finger-lickin' good rather than a leading cause of mass death).

Those who got through the trials alive but with a belly full of chicken skin, having failed to throw them up, could not expect good things. If you were guilty of a crime, were a Christian, hadn't paid taxes, or just weren't a big fan of Ranavalona for some reason (can't imagine why) you were likely to end up starving to death in prison, or in slavery.

Ranavalona continued to look back to bygone years for inspiration for punishments. Like how your dad refuses to give up his Nokia 3310, she refused to stop doing the medieval torture practices of boiling people alive in oil, tying them down and burning them, or just burying them alive and leaving them there like a screaming time capsule.

In 1845, in what was clearly meant to be some sort of redeeming fun trip to make up for all the killing, Ranavalona organised a hunt, sending about fifty thousand subjects, servants and slaves out to capture some buffalo. Probably thinking, 'She is definitely going to make us eat buffalo skins, isn't she, I'm not sure I can cope with vomiting three whole buffalo skins,' the people of Madagascar set out on their jaunt. In order to get to the buffalo, slaves were forced to build the roads as they went, making their way through the dense jungle (always read the small print). For four months Ranavalona's subjects continued the hunt. By the time they were finished, about ten thousand had died from malaria, exhaustion or hunger, and not a single buffalo was killed. Which I guess, from the perspective of the buffalo, was fantastic.

Ranavalona's brutal reign, during which even a friendly hunt came with a higher death toll than Ebola, ended when she passed away in her sleep in 1861. Before her son (who would do away with her kill-frenzy ways and, in the process, highlight that she was an asshole rather than merely a product of time and circumstances) could take the throne, a spark set a barrel of gunpowder alight at her funeral, killing a whole pile of mourners. But, in a way, that's exactly what she would have wanted.

THE EXECUTIONER WHO WAS NOTORIOUSLY BAD AT EXECUTIONS

As a general rule, anybody who voluntarily becomes an executioner is probably a bit of a wrong 'un. In the whole of human history, nobody has ever remarked, 'You have to meet my lovely friend, he likes to sever the heads and spines of humans for money and he is a delight!' So to really distinguish yourself as an asshole in the field of executioners is quite the feat, like being the worst Rees-Mogg. However, Jack Ketch, who worked as King Charles II's executioner from 1663 to 1686, stood out from the pack, no trouble.

Following his apprenticeship (yes, he was genuinely an apprentice – it's not like you can take an A level in head-chopping theory and then apply for jobs), he began work, perfecting the art of hanging, drawing, quartering and gibbeting. Of this work there were no complaints, probably because you don't want to annoy someone with that skillset.

However, Ketch wasn't particularly well liked, for several reasons. He had a fondness for drinking heavily at work – though, to be fair, there weren't many people in his business, and maybe ripping out people's guts for display paired well with a Merlot. He also liked to squeeze as much cash as possible out of his clients before they were executed, offering quicker and less painful deaths to those who would bribe him handsomely. Though this was apparently fine at the time, he did it so often and took so much in bribe money that people thought he was taking the piss.[1] (Also, side note, but the executioner was allowed to keep the clothes of the deceased as a perk, like a company car, which probably made him even more unlikeable.)

Though most of the executions Jack performed were via hanging, it was with his axe that he really found his infamy. In times gone by, due to a lack of practice in England, an executioner from Europe would be called in to perform beheadings, to make sure they were quick and clean. Not so in the case of William, Lord Russell, who Ketch was called upon to execute for treason in 1683. Ketch offered his usual bribe of charging people more to guarantee he do his job properly – a tactic I'm sorely tempted by, myself – before setting Russell up at the block.

The execution was horrendously botched, with Ketch first catching Russell in the shoulder, before taking several more blows to finish him off. All for thirty guineas (about £3,100 in today's money), though if Russell had a problem with that it's not like he could have taken it up with customer services. Accounts say that Ketch had either botched it deliberately (I suppose the problem with the job of executioner is you tend to attract assholes) or that he was just drunk, with the execution forming just a small part of his day on the lash.

The execution was so bad, with Russell suffering excruciating pain, that the crowd were outraged – a crowd, I might add, that saw some guy getting his head chopped off as a cultured day out. In response, Ketch ended up publishing an apology leaflet[2] in which he blamed Russell, saying that Russell had failed to 'dispose himself as was most suitable', or, in other words, had failed to keep his head in the right position while a fucking axe was being swung at his neck.

The next of Ketch's axe executions was that of James Scott, 1st Duke of Monmouth in 1685, again for treason. Scott took a slightly better precaution than Russell, only part-paying Ketch for a clean execution, with a promise of more from his servant if he did a good job. 'Do not serve me as you did my Lord Russell. I have heard you struck him three or four times,'[3] he told Ketch, before asking whether his blade was sharp enough.

Perhaps not liking a backseat executioner, when it came to the date of the execution, Ketch delivered a first blow so bad that it caused Scott to turn his head around and look at him in annoyance. I realise you may not be familiar with how executions go, but if the executed is tutting at you, chances are you've done a bad job.

Ketch then started hacking away at Scott's neck, each time causing him immense pain, but failing to deliver a fatal blow. He then threw down his weapon in a sulk and refused to finish the job, even though being an executioner is very much one of those jobs where you can't put off completing your task till tomorrow or after lunch. The sheriff at the scene had to then threaten Ketch in order to get him to finish the execution, while Scott lay there with half his neck hanging off. He had another two goes, before giving up with the axe and removing the rest of the head using a knife he had to hand.

Following the botched executions, Ketch's name briefly became slang for 'Satan', which can't have filled him with confidence for the next job. Fortunately for his victims, he was convicted of affronting a sheriff and sent to jail, though he first sent his own assistant in his place. Like if you won a place on the American *Apprentice* and the first task was to appear in front of Congress to be impeached on behalf of Donald Trump. However, his assistant ended up getting hanged for another crime (clearly, all the executions he'd helped carry out weren't enough of a deterrent to stop him from committing crimes), and so Ketch was sent to jail, where he died shortly afterwards. At least he was spared the excruciating pain of being executed by himself.

THE DOCTOR WHO TRIED TO MAKE A HUMANZEE

There are certain people who should never be told to follow their dreams. Hitler, for example. Or anybody who longs to one day grow up, study science and get a human and an ape together in order to create a humanzee. Unfortunately, nobody sat down Ilya Ivanovich Ivanov in his youth and told him to give up.

Ivanov was a Russian biologist born in 1870 who was spectacularly good at his job, which happened to be animal artificial insemination. Look, someone's got to do it and Ivanov was really, really good at wanking off a horse and then implanting the semen into a second horse. It was said that he could inseminate five hundred mares[1] with the semen of just one stallion, which is impressive on the parts of both the scientist and the horse for producing such a vast volume of jizz.

As is inevitable when you're at the top of your game, the mind starts to wander and you look for new challenges to keep you entertained. For footballers, it's probably something like kicking a slightly larger ball (I'm guessing here; footballers are not the most imaginative people I've ever met). For Ivanov, it was getting the sperm out of new animals and putting it into different species to see what happened. Like when you bake a cake but don't quite follow a recipe (but with a significant amount more jizz. One hopes.)

Ivanov's first attempts were pretty vanilla. He began by creating the zedonk (a mix between a zebra and a donkey) before moving on to a rat-mouse (the clue is in the name) and a cross between an antelope and a cow, which the melon didn't even have the imagination to name a fucking cantelope.

Like a serial killer moving on from practising on dogs, his mind soon turned to humans. Also, to be fair to him, maybe he had merely grown weary of wanking off mice. In 1910, Ivanov began telling scientific colleagues that he believed it would be possible to mix a human with a chimp.[2] They believed he was talking hypothetically, as other scientists had done in the past, and this is how nobody discovered in his lab a little jar labelled something along the lines of 'Curious George cum'.

For years, nobody would fund his project. But after the Russian Revolution of 1917, he managed to secure funding. Amazingly (I say amazingly mainly because I can't imagine how ballsy you'd have to be to say 'Can I have some money – I want to put some human jizz in an ape') he received $10,000 from the Soviet Financial Commission to carry out his work,[3] before securing the approval of the Soviet Academy of Sciences, as well as senior members of the Bolshevik government. Many layers of government sat there and went 'Hairy ape boy – sounds perfect. FETCH THE STAMP OF APPROVAL, SHEILA.' The Bolsheviks – the revolutionary Marxist party founded by Vladimir Lenin – had a vested interest in proving the theory of evolution, as it would be a blow against their arch-nemesis, organised religion. This might partly explain why they were willing to let Ivanov have a crank on some monkeys.

In 1926, Ivanov and an equally depraved colleague transplanted a human ovary into an ape, and then attempted to inseminate her using human sperm. We don't know whose, but I would hazard a guess that if you think producing monkey men is fine, you're probably not above it being yours or just one of your pals'. Every time, it failed.

Too far down the path to admit defeat, Ivanov decided to take a much worse approach. He set about taking sperm from chimps, which he planned to place inside African women in French Guinea (now Guinea), where he had the support of the Pasteur Institute, who ran an ape sanctuary there. This would be done without the women's knowledge or consent, by getting doctors to pretend they were giving them a medical examination, when really they were being inseminated. Had the plan succeeded, the mothers would probably have found out what had happened only when their baby came out with a suspicious knack for climbing and an exceptional amount of hair coverage.

The governor in charge of French Guinea, thank god, was not a fan of the idea, and Ivanov was not allowed to go ahead. He instead decided to recruit women in the Soviet Union who were willing to give birth to a humanzee. Somehow – and honestly I would like to see how this guy pitched it, because it can't have been an easy sell and he clearly fucking nailed the presentation – he found over five women who were willing to give it a go.

Disaster struck, in that the chimpanzees he was keeping for his deranged experiment – in what was quite a canny move on behalf of the apes – died. Completely out of monkey jizz, Ivanov tried to ship in more, but in the meantime the Soviet Academy of Sciences decided to end the project, not on moral grounds, but over a lack of cum.

Before he could find a new way to complete his project, Ivanov was sentenced to exile in a purge of scientists – part of Stalin's attempt to be rid of Leninists – before he could even explain that he was 'just the jizz guy'.

CHRISTOPHER COLUMBUS

For centuries, Christopher Columbus lucked out in the reputation department, with some people (more commonly known as 'Americans') still thinking of him as a hero today. Among the populations of people he didn't slaughter or sell, he gained a reputation as the man who explored the Americas, and proved the Earth was round, even though people had known about this for centuries before he set sail on his voyage of atrocities in 1492. In fact, after sailing the world he came to believe it was shaped like a pear, or 'una teta de muger allí puesta', or a big ball with a gigantic nipple on it in the east.[1] This is why you should never speculate on the shape of the Earth while horny.

On day one of landing in the New World, during the voyage of 1492 on behalf of the King of Spain, Columbus captured six Native Americans, the first of thousands to be forced into labour – a prototype for the systematic slavery that was to come in the following centuries. He and his administration also took and sold sex slaves. In one particularly grim passage in his writings, he describes how 'a hundred castellanoes [coins] are as easily obtained for a woman as for a farm, and it is very general and there are plenty of dealers who go about looking for girls; those from nine to ten are now in demand',[2] comparing the capture of nine-year-olds for sex slavery to the sale of a bit of land.

Though the quote doesn't make explicit that Columbus was personally involved in trading people of such a young age, one such associate – Michele de Cuneo, who joined him on his second expedition to the Americas – told of how he had been gifted a female slave by Columbus. He then launched into an anecdote about how he had to break her spirit by whipping her with a rope, until 'eventually we came to such terms, I assure you, that you would have thought she had been brought up in a school for whores'.[3] Which, I'd argue, is the kind of anecdote that should prevent the gifter from having his own national day, if the US could look into that pretty sharpish.

Columbus, like a villain in one of the earlier Bond movies, was also a huge fan of gold. He mandated that the Taíno people – who occupied the area that is now Haiti and the Dominican Republic – hand over gold as tribute to him and his administrators. The penalty for the crime of not giving him enough shiny things was that they would have one of their hands cut off.[4] Given the lack of medical knowledge at the time, this would often result in them bleeding to death, making their next tribute somewhat difficult to cough up.

Columbus' reign was so brutal that it led to many thousands of deaths. In Hispaniola (now the Dominican Republic), thousands of locals committed suicide rather than face life under him. Some destroyed their own stores of food to prevent the occupiers from eating it. Unfortunately this meant they also had no food for themselves. Estimates of population numbers upon Columbus' arrival vs fifty-six years later put it at three hundred thousand vs five hundred. The practice of making locals pay tributes of gold (or cotton, in areas where gold wasn't available) contributed to mass starvation, giving them no metal to trade for food and less time to actually grow any.

To be fair to Columbus, he was a terrible asshole to his own shipmates and fellow colonialists as well, and regularly executed people for minor crimes, once cutting out the tongue of a woman for saying that he was the son of a weaver.[5] Which he was. One boy, who pulled up a trap that didn't belong to him from a river to catch a fish, shortly thereafter found his hand nailed to the floor where he'd caught it, which is only justice from the point of view of the most hardline of fish.

Defenders of Columbus might say something along the lines of 'He wasn't evil by the standards of his time'. Well, first up, congratulations for defending a man who cut the hands off of people who couldn't give him enough gold. I hope you're proud of yourself. Secondly, he was so terrible in his governing that in 1500 the King and Queen of Spain sent a royal administrator to bring him back to Spain,[6] where he couldn't do any more damage.

In summary, rather than the heroic explorer he has sometimes been portrayed as, Columbus was a ruthless bigot responsible for many thousands of deaths, who fervently believed the earth was shaped like a tit.

THE MAN WHO GOT THREE JESUSES AND MADE THEM FIGHT

In 1959 in Ypsilanti, Michigan, a psychologist by the name of Milton Rokeach got three people who believed they were the one true Jesus and just sort of let them fight it out amongst themselves. All of the men had been diagnosed with schizophrenia, and had the kind of identity problems that wouldn't be helped by arranging a kind of grudge match with people who also believed they were the Messiah. Nevertheless, Rokeach, having been inspired by a similar situation involving two women who thought they were the Virgin Mary, believed that the way to cure these men was to hook them up and see if the presence of two other Jesuses would cure them of their own belief that they were the one true Jesus.

The first few meetings went about as well as you would expect, in that the three Jesuses actively hated each other. They broke character to call each other bitches and threaten each other with things like 'I'm gonna kill you – you son of a bitch!' when one of the Jesuses, Leon, claimed that Clyde, one of the other Jesuses, had a foster father who was a sandpiper (a type of bird). It's unclear why this would be an insult worthy of a death threat to all but the most violent of ornithologists.

Undeterred, Rokeach continued the experiments for another two years. Each man remained convinced that he was the true Jesus, and found reasons to explain away the other two Jesuses. Clyde believed the other two to be dead automatons, sort of like a pair of animatronic Jesuses. Leon, who was far less confrontational than the others, believed the other two were lesser gods, and occasionally the reincarnated souls of King Mathius and Captain Davy Jones. Joseph – the third Jesus – believed himself to be God, and that the other two were 'patients in a mental hospital' and their being patients proved they were 'insane'.[1] All of them believed that they had created the other two, which became a bit of a bone of contention the more the experiment went on.

Far from realising they couldn't be Jesus, each Jesus sometimes descended into attempting to pummel the shit out of the other two Jesuses to claim the Jesus throne. The first actual fist-fight broke out when Leon claimed that Adam was his own brother-in-law (he wasn't). Clyde went full Jesus-in-the-temple and punched Leon in the face, while Leon didn't react, going with a Jesus-turns-the-other-cheek approach.

It soon became clear to Rokeach that the project, as it was, wasn't really working, at which point he dabbled in a bit of good old-fashioned mental torture. Of the three, Leon was having the most psychological issues, and became convinced that he had a wife called Madame Yeti Woman. Rather than, for instance, saying 'No you don't' and offering Leon proper therapy, Rokeach began sending letters to him, pretending to be Yeti Woman, claiming to be in love with him and arranging to meet him for several dates. Given that she existed about as much as an actual yeti, this became somewhat problematic. Leon would show up to the dates within the grounds of the hospital, and find no one there, at which point he would become distressed and agitated. Then, when Yeti Woman began to express doubt that he was Jesus in her letters, Leon figured out he was being played and became withdrawn.

At last Rokeach learned his lesson, which he believed to be 'You have to hire an actual woman if you're going to fuck around with someone's feelings like this', and so he did. One of Rokeach's research assistants pretended to be attracted to Leon, eventually getting him to fall in love with her, before he again figured out he was being punked. Sure the experiment was fucking pointless, but hey, Rokeach was practically the forerunner of prank TV by this point.

Before the experiment was over, the three Jesuses became better friends once they stopped talking about the elephant in the room. They had a lot in common after all. The only alteration in their identities was that Leon stopped asking to be referred to as the Messiah, preferring instead to go by Dr Righteous Idealized Dung[2] – which isn't exactly what I'd call progress – and he continued to believe that he was still Jesus, but now a Jesus with self-worth issues.

Rokeach, after his assistants disavowed the project on the grounds that it was cruel, accepted the experiment had been a failure, and later admitted that he had no right to play God.

PETER THE GREAT

There must be a lot of pressure on kings and queens to not fuck things up. Don't get me wrong – this is more than made up for by the diamond hats and all the swans you can own, but it must grate on you to know that, should you screw things up in some way, you could be forever stuck with a crap suffix, like Ethelred the Unready, or Henry the Impotent, or simply be forever known as 'the Bastard'.

Keep your head down too much, though, and you get listed for something shit. There are genuinely five kings in Europe who got stuck with the suffix 'the Bearded' as if that was their defining characteristic. All that work trying to not be as memorable or douchey as Peter the Cruel and in the end everyone sees you as some sort of fucking beard stand.

Peter the Great of Russia was one of the lucky ones because, in truth, he probably should have been named 'Peter the ... look, some of the stuff he did was OK, but there is the old head-pickling thing which we probably need to discuss'.

Peter was born in 1672 and ascended to the Russian throne just ten years later. He jointly ruled with his older brother until 1696, sharing the whole of Russia like a deck of Pokémon cards. Coming to the throne at that age could have been a disaster, but Peter was actually quite good at it, using a lot of his time to modernise Russia, industrialising it and bringing in popular reforms such as allowing townspeople to elect their own municipalities rather than be ruled by military governors.

Meanwhile, his personal life was a shitshow. He divorced his first wife, Eudoxia Lopukhina, at twenty-six, and forced her to join a convent. You think modern-day divorces are bad – imagine losing the dog, and also you're now a nun.

Complicating things somewhat was their son Alexis, who had taken the trouble to not die like his two siblings had, meaning he would have a future claim to the throne. Alexis, who was against many of his father's reforms, was pressured by his father to become a monk in order to give up the claim, but he chose instead to flee to Austria for the protection of Holy Roman Emperor Charles VI in 1716. A few years later, he came back to Russia, where he was promptly tortured and sentenced to death, then killed in prison before chop-chop time.

Peter's second wife was a bit more of a love story than that (I know it's not difficult to beat a murder of a child and a nunning, but still) with the obvious exception of the ending. Peter met Marta Helena Skowrońska between 1702 and 1704, at his best friend's house, where she worked as a servant. She was the daughter of, according to conflicting accounts, a farmer, a gravedigger, an officer or a handyman. She was a peasant and not someone whom the aristocracy would see as fit to marry an emperor. Despite this, Peter fell in love with her wit, and Marta converted to the Russian Orthodox Church – changing her name to Catherine – in order to marry Peter, with whom she went on to have twelve children.[1]

This is the point where Disney would have placed the 'happily ever after' placard, skipping out the bit where they both started banging other people, one of whom became a gherkin. Peter had several mistresses in his time, including one Anna Mons. Anna had a brother called Willem who became close to Catherine, and there were rumours of a relationship between the two. The whole situation was pretty icky, a sort of incest via proxy, but was about to get much worse. Despite more than a little hypocrisy (he was mad at his wife rawdogging the brother of the woman he was banging), Peter had Willem charged with taking bribes, leading to his public execution, whereupon Peter kept his head and pickled it in a jar of spirits.[2]

There are rumours that Peter gave Catherine the head as a sort of memento, or made her keep it by her bed as a warning to other potential lovers who could still maintain an erection while doing it in front of a head in a jar. She kept the jar until her own death, so perhaps the first one is true. What's known is that pickling the head of someone who may have just been Catherine's friend put a strain on their relationship somewhat. They began to eat meals separately, and spoke a lot less in the following three months until Peter died of a bladder illness and cirrhosis. And somehow he didn't get remembered as Peter The What The Fuck Are You Doing With That Massive Jar?

THE EGG SMASHERS OF SAN FRANCISCO

After gold was found in California in the 1840s, San Francisco grew exponentially. Hundreds of thousands of miners would travel through the city every year, on their way to mine gold. The expansion of the city came with its own challenges. Of all the problems people migrating to the city hadn't anticipated, a lack of omelettes was way up there. Farmers were unable to instantly up their produce to match demand, leading to a severe lack of proteins available in the city. This resulted in the mad price of a dollar per egg (about £24 in today's money).[1] Basically, imagine waiting for payday to have a big night out, but instead you're now going to spend it indoors eating a single egg for dinner.

However, this was a time of entrepreneurs, the American spirit, and dicks, and the problem wasn't going to last long. On the nearby Farallon Islands, there lived hundreds of thousands of seabirds that laid eggs not too dissimilar from chicken eggs. During 'egg season', murre birds laid big turquoise eggs, which would fry well, even if they did stay translucent. Side note, but if you think that's gross I say this: you're eating bird periods – stop being so fussy. Did it cross a line that your bird period is see-through? What is wrong with your standards?

The eggs were there for the taking, and that's exactly what 'eggers' did. Now, when you hear someone is an 'egger' for a living, you probably don't picture a big burly man with several shotguns and a look in his eyes like he's seen some serious shit. But you should, if you know what's good for you. The first eggers had to contend with collecting the eggs from shit-covered cliffs, which was no small feat, and led to several deaths. But when word got around about how lucrative the egg business was – these birds were literally shitting money out of their cloacae – the business got even more dangerous than before. Several gangs of rival eggers headed to the island, and year after year there was the kind of violence you wouldn't expect to have to carry out just to make your eggs Florentine. Several different egg factions staked their claim on the island, and then had turf wars, as you would have among your bog-standard crack dealers. In 1860, police were sent to arrest one group of eggers, only to find 'two parties, armed to the teeth, in possession of different parts of the island, and breathing defiance against each other'.[2]

Fights, stabbings and shootings, injuries and murders, hijackings and boat fights (all, I imagine, delivered while making egg puns – the only ones of which I can think of are too terrible to be recorded in writing) became so commonplace that the US government stepped in, and gave one group monopoly over the island. They actually had to do this, as the courts were becoming clogged up with egg crime. This group became known as the Pacific Egg Company.

However, though the company had been given rights to the eggs, the wars were far from over. The Pacific Egg Company decided to fight the lighthouse keepers who also inhabited the island, and generally tried to mind their own business. They banned the keepers from taking any of the eggs, which was pretty much the only source of food to be found on what was still mostly an eggy island. When one of the lighthouse keepers ignored the order, they were, of course, attacked by the company.

The fight for Eggy Island wasn't won or lost through violence in the end, but through economics. Eventually, chicken farmers got their act together and came to San Francisco, driving down the price of chicken eggs as well as the demand for fishy-tasting eggs covered in a suspicious amount of human blood and misery. Another drawback was that the eggs remained translucent when cooked, which is, at best, a bit icky. Nevertheless, as they scrambled to get the last bit of profit out of the eggs, some eggers still had to be removed by the fucking military.

During their time, eggers had moved around fourteen million (now) rare murre eggs to San

Francisco, for cakes that likely tasted like shit. What's worse was that the first thing that the eggers did when arriving on the island for egging season was to smash every egg in sight, ensuring that all the eggs they collected from then on would be as fresh as possible, because all prior eggs were in pieces on what used to be a nice eggy island.

THE VARIED ABUSERS OF OOFTY GOOFTY

When you hear the name Oofty Goofty, it's a safe assumption that the person who holds it has had a fairly unusual life. You rarely, for instance, hear the phrase 'I'd like you to meet our top performer Oofty Goofty' at an induction session at work, unless you happen to be some sort of fucking clown.

Oofty didn't always go by this name, however. He was born as Leonard Borchardt in Germany on 26 April 1862, before moving to San Francisco as an adult. Desperate for work, and having fled the army, he hit upon some luck when he found a street circus in need of a new act. Well, I say 'luck'. A few moments later the circus-owner 'took me to his room, where he took some stray human hairs from an old mattress, and after having made me strip he stuck it all over me with some kind of glue which he said he had discovered'. For a share of the ticket sales, Leonard would be required to be covered in the experimental glue and a shitload of other people's hair, and act like a fucking Neanderthal. Members of the circus would feed him raw meat through the bars and customers would give him beer, while his job was to run around like a 'wild man' and yell 'OOFTY GOOFTY' over and over again through the bars. If that wasn't bad enough, before Leonard had even finished his probation, his manager told him he had already drunk his share of the payment, so Leonard wouldn't be getting any actual money.

The gig did not last long. According to a report in the *San Francisco Chronicle*, police had to intervene when Oofty became sick, unable to breathe through his hairy tar coat. He was taken to hospital, where doctors spent days trying to peel it off without his flesh being torn away, before eventually leaving him on the roof for several more days in the blazing hot sun, in an attempt to get the tar-like substance to melt off Oofty's skin.

Although he had only been the sideshow act at the circus for a week, the name Oofty Goofty stuck, like some ass hair glued to a deserter's face. This is like being named after the most humiliating moment of your life. Imagine getting married and the priest asks 'Do you, Once Shat Herself In The Office After Contracting Salmonella, take this man, Was Wanking In The Shower When His Nan Walked In, to be your lawfully wedded husband?'

Life was about to get worse for Mr Goofty, however, as he now had about the same amount of job as he did dignity. For a time, he was employed as a mascot for a baseball team, but after they kept losing he was fired, and they abandoned him in the middle of nowhere to walk home from a hundred miles away. Then, in a desperate attempt to win a bet that he couldn't mail himself to Sacramento, he mailed himself to Sacramento,[1] in a package that the mail workers placed upside down, cutting off a lot of his airholes.

After getting violently rejected from job after job and taking several beatings from various potential employers (back then, apparently, they would tell you it was close but you didn't make the cut by merely hurling you out of the establishment onto the rocks below, rather than today's much more hurtful ghosting) he hit upon an idea: he would allow people to beat him for money.

This is where a whole new stream of assholes come into the story. You would like to think that if someone saw a man, down on his luck and offering people a range of prices to beat the shit out of him, they might, at the very least, walk on by without stopping to chin him. Not the case in San Francisco, where Oofty could make a living letting people twat him with a small cane for ten cents, or pay two dollars to swing at him with a fucking baseball bat.

For a time, Oofty managed to make a comfortable living out of this, and was saving up money to go back home to Germany, a country whose inhabitants wouldn't pay to smack him around, when he was sued for libel (he had claimed, with no apparent good reason other than he too was a bit of an asshole, that a man by the name of C. Linear had paid him to burn a house down) and had to start all over again.

He then decided to start performing stunts for paying crowds, such as trying to push a wheelbarrow over extraordinary distances, but found gangs of youths would fight him for his wheelbarrow. He finally stopped pushing the wheelbarrow when somebody pushed him into the river,[2] really letting him know how the wheelbarrow must have felt.

Oofty never managed to return to Germany, and spent his later years telling people his story, and betting them $50 that he wouldn't cry if they hit him with a drill. But when your life has been that awful because of the surrounding assholes, it's not so impressive that you no longer have the capacity to feel feelings.

SAINT OLGA OF KIEV

There are many routes to becoming a saint. They generally involve doing some sort of miracle or, at the very least, coming across as quite smug. Olga of Kiev took secret option number three: burning every last one of her enemies to the ground.

Olga was married to Igor, Prince of Kiev, when in 945 AD he attacked a neighbouring tribe of Early East Slavs, the Drevlians – something he would live to regret. Fortunately he didn't have to regret it for long, as they soon captured him and executed him via tree: his enemies took his legs and tied them to two separate birch trees that had been bent down towards him from the top.[1] When the trees were released they sprang back up and tore him in two from the penis and testicles right up to his face. As if the pain wasn't bad enough, before you were cut in two you were briefly made to do the splits, like your execution had been choreographed by Louie Spence.

Igor's son and heir was only three – far too young to make the kind of grown-up decisions that kings should make, especially as such decisions could potentially result in you being ripped apart from asshole to face. Fortunately, his mother Olga was on hand to make all the decisions for him, and so the killing spree began.

Having removed Igor from the picture, the Drevlians decided that they quite fancied some extra power and territory, and planned to marry Olga to their leader, Prince Mal. This wasn't exactly a winner of an idea for Olga, given that Mal had placed the order for her previous husband to be executed. At best you'd be looking at some incredibly tense pillow talk during the honeymoon period.

Mal sent twenty of his best men to meet her with his proposal, maybe sensing that 'Hi, I'm that guy that made your husband's penis fly one way while a lot of his teeth went the other' wasn't a great opener. When they arrived, Olga greeted the men, and for a time it seemed to be going a lot better than the Drevlians anticipated. 'Your proposal is pleasing to me; indeed my husband cannot rise again from the dead. But I desire to honour you tomorrow in the presence of my people,' Olga is said to have told them. 'Return now to your boat, and remain there with an aspect of arrogance. I shall send for you on the morrow, and you shall say, "We will not ride on horses nor go on foot; carry us in our boat." And you shall be carried in your boat.'[2]

They left for the evening, and Olga ordered her servants to dig a gigantic hole in her court. The next day, probably feeling like idiots, Mal's men returned and demanded to be carried in their boats to see Olga. After a bit of awkward land-surfing (after all, what do you say to someone who is carrying you in a boat? 'So, you ever done this with a barge?'), they arrived in Olga's hall – and were immediately thrown in the hole, where Olga ordered that they should be buried alive.

Olga insisted the problem was that Mal had sent her men who were substandard – such absolute rejects that she had no choice but to boat the cunts into the dirt. She insisted that Mal send her better men, and so he sent the rulers of Iskorosten – the Drevlians' principal city and what is now Korosten in northern Ukraine – to propose instead. When they arrived, probably wondering how they were meant to meet her on top of the bodies of their predecessors, she invited them to clean themselves up in the bathhouse before she greeted them. Making the classic mistake of putting their swords away, getting their dicks out and going for a dip, they found the doors to the bathhouse were closed behind them and immediately set on fire.

Next, Olga, along with her army, travelled to Iskorosten and held it under siege, though if their leaders were anything to go by, there's a good chance that when she showed up and began slaying everyone in sight, a lot of the Iskorostens' last words were probably 'Proposal seems to be going swell, do I hear wedding bells?' before she ripped out their spines by hand.

After a long siege, Olga declared that she had forgiven them, and they should gather up a large amount of mead and take it to where they executed her husband. Here, she would drink mead and commemorate him. Of course, this was an ambush and she massacred five thousand morons who had turned up with beer to a knife fight.

Olga then declared that she'd completed her rampage, and would end the siege if the Iskorostens sent her a small tribute. Rather than gold, furs or more mead, she asked only that they each send three pigeons and three sparrows, given how impoverished they'd become by the siege.

The problem was, the Iskorostens were in possession of lots of lovely flammable wood. Probably thrilled that Olga had asked for the shittest of all the birds rather than the wood (to be fair, they should have realised what this was foreshadowing), they complied with her request. Knowing that the pigeons and sparrows would return to their nests in the roofs of the wooden houses, Olga ordered her soldiers to attach sulphur to the birds via a small pouch. Being extremely flammable, the sulphur caught fire and Iskorosten burned to the ground overnight, with every last inhabitant either burned with it, killed as they fled, or enslaved afterwards.

Mal probably took this as a maybe.

IVAN THE TERRIBLE

JOB TITLE
Oprichniki officer

JOB DESCRIPTION
Cause havoc/terror on behalf of Tsar Ivan

JOB REQUIREMENTS
Must have experience in causing terror on wide scale

Must have proven experience in executions

Must be generally all-round terrible person

Must own severed pig head

Now I don't want to heap too much praise on Ivan for reasons that will become clear, but it's objectively impressive to murder your own son and still come away with a nickname on a par with Ivan The Loveable Scamp. He was helped somewhat by the translation into English making it sound less evil. The more accurate (though cumbersome) translation is Ivan The Inspirer Of Terror, which his deeds definitely justified.

Ivan – born 25 August 1530 – didn't have the best start in life, despite being Grand Prince of Moscow. A quick glance at history shows us that royals live their childhood either in absolute luxury, or locked away in a room like a forgotten tin of beans as part of some sort of power move. Ivan's childhood involved the latter.

After the death of his father, Ivan technically should have ascended to the throne. However, being of such a young age at the time – he was only three – he was very much under the thumb of the local aristocracy, who were supposed to be preparing him to rule. However, the aristocracy had no intention of raising Ivan to become a powerful leader, so instead they locked him up – often in confined spaces – and beat him mercilessly.[1] Then, when he was eight, his mother was poisoned to death, possibly by a rival family – the Shuiskys – who wanted to seize power for themselves. In order to survive, Ivan made friends with some of his captors, gaining more freedoms and support through his alliances.

Eventually, over the next few decades, he was able to negotiate absolute power over the aristocracy who had locked him away for so long, which meant he could now kill them if he had a free afternoon and no admin to be getting on with. In 1565 he established the Oprichniki – a group of paid bodyguards and thugs who would ride around doing his bidding, with severed pigs heads attached to their saddles.[2]

Think of a private police force, but the officers have a big ham stapled to their lapels. The Oprichniki were encouraged to execute anybody who wasn't on board with Ivan's regime, a regime that was especially hard to be enthusiastic about seeing as Ivan essentially authorised the boiling, impaling and roasting of people to death on a spit.[3]

Over the next few years, Ivan became increasingly paranoid. This in combination with an army of ruthless killers at your disposal is not a great mix. (Rarely have I seen a person deep in paranoia, telling me that their enemies are everywhere, and thought, 'Get this man some killers, stat.') But Ivan the Terrible had both. In probably the worst part of his reign, he used the Oprichniki to carry out a massacre in the Russian city of Novgorod in 1570.

Novgorod had once been independent, but by now fell within Ivan's domain. He believed – probably wrongly – that it was favourable towards the Polish king, a king that, crucially, wasn't him. The city had gone through a number of famines in recent years, and did not put up a fight when Ivan arrived with his army of pig boys, letting them make their way inside the city.[4] Novgorod surrendered completely, and Ivan then made sure that the inhabitants were punished for their imagined crimes. It's unclear how many were killed – estimates range from two to fifteen thousand – but during the month-long murder-fest, priests were flogged and beaten to death, women and children murdered, and men thrown into the icy river and killed if they tried to escape.[5]

Ivan definitely had a thirst for violence, which only got worse as his reign went on – perhaps due to the large amounts of mercury he was ingesting for various ailments, as was the style at the time, of which symptoms included nervousness, anxiety, irritability and mood swings. He also attracted a lot of strange rumours and myths. Legend has it that when St Basil's Cathedral in Moscow was completed in 1560, he loved it so much that he gouged out the eyes of the designer, so that he could never create anything as beautiful ever again. Apart from anything else, this can't have been a great motivator for any of his subsequent contractors. Imagine being his chef, having a taste of the king's Bolognese, before realising 'I'd better make this a bit shitter if I want to keep my tongue' and frantically googling Jamie Oliver recipes.

The legend is unlikely to be true, given that he hired the same guy to design other buildings afterwards, which you're unlikely to do with someone you've just personally blinded, but it's a little bit telling that it's the sort of thing people easily believed about Ivan, in the way that you would never believe, e.g. David Attenborough punches moles just to feel alive.

In the years before his death in 1584, Ivan would fly into violent rages on a regular basis. During one such bout of the angries, he killed his own son with a blow to the head.[6] His boy had confronted him for beating his wife and causing her to have a miscarriage, which Ivan had done because he didn't like her clothes that day. That's a lot of death for a fashion faux pas, and there could have been real carnage if he had ever attended Paris Fashion Week.

THE BEAR TRAINER WHO WASN'T TOO FUSSED IF YOU WERE OR WEREN'T A BEAR

In the late eighteenth century, Irish priest Arthur O'Leary was walking along the beach of Boulogne-sur-Mer, a name so French it would feel patronising to mention it is in France, when he happened upon a huge crowd. They were gathered around and making the kinds of noises one might make when being entertained by a dancing bear.

The bear at the centre of the ruckus was on a leash and performing tricks for the crowd. As this was the late eighteenth century, the priest didn't really note that anything was that unusual, other than the bear was exceptionally well trained. The beach was crammed full of dangerous animals doing performances in those days, probably. Go to put a towel down and you'd have to shift at least three performing black mambas.

O'Leary returned every day of his stay to the beach, where he saw the bear doing suspiciously good tricks. As well as dancing, if you waved at the bear, it would give a friendly nod in return. If you handed it a clock face, it could point to what the time was, even though bears have no business being anywhere at a pre-arranged hour.

The bear was hot shit, and people came from miles away to watch it. There was nothing people loved more back then than a tied-up wild animal nodding and pointing at clocks.

But on day four of O'Leary's beach trips, the bear appeared a lot more reluctant than normal.[1] It refused to do tricks, and kept on trying to lie down for a nap. The trainer, the esteemed asshole of this chapter, began to prod the bear with a sharp stick, putting himself in grave danger of being the guy behind the 'don't poke the bear' phrase.

The bear began making loud, threatening and incomprehensible bear sounds, at least if you happened to not be from Ireland. However, Arthur knew that the bear had in fact shouted, in perfect Gaelic, '*T'anam ón Diabhal, táim cráite go deo leis an buc seoo*', or 'The devil take him, this guy has me persecuted'.[2] To further translate into modern English, it's something along the lines of 'Go to hell, this dickhead has sewn me into a bear costume!' for that is exactly what had happened. Somewhat surprised that the bear could talk, and that it wasn't speaking French, O'Leary asked in Gaelic, 'How are you, dear?' to which the bear responded, 'Very well, thank you,' which under the circumstances was both great and fucking terrifying.

O'Leary marched the bear and trainer to see the mayor of the town of Boulogne-sur-Mer, a sentence practically begging for a children's picture book about the whole debacle. In front of the mayor, the priest and the bear began chatting, at which point the trainer realised that the jig was up, dropped the leash and pegged it.

The bear was actually a man from a famine-stricken area of Waterford in Ireland, who had taken a job on a ship to escape. The boat had been wrecked, and the man had floated to the shore of a strange land, that strangest of lands being northern France, whereupon he had looked for help and been sewn into a bear costume by a trainer and forced to perform for food.

Details are scarce on how the man had been sewn into his costume, so I shall offer some theories:

1) He arrived on the shore completely unconscious. He woke up, confused, and looked down at his paws. Terrified, he sought for help, but a Frenchman just said, '*Danse.*'

2) He arrived on the shore conscious and alarmed. He asked for help, and was wrestled into a costume while he tried to remember his GCSE French. Before his voice was muffled, he managed to splutter out '*Où est la bibliothèque?*', earning him three pokes from the bear-poking stick.

The costume was likely not at all convincing, but the captor was probably relying on poor French villagers never having seen a bear. At the time, it wasn't like they could google what bears really looked like, so many of them would have come away thinking, 'Ah so that's a bear, is it – tiny, hairy, sleepy little Irish fella who likes to dance on cue.'

Following the revelation that the bear was in fact an Irishman, he was removed from his costume and allowed to go free. Before he did so, he was asked why he didn't protest about his situation, and he replied that he didn't mind so much, as at least he was being fed. And on the bright side, whenever he did some normal human thing such as tell the time or just nod, people would lose their shit in a way you probably haven't experienced since you were three, getting applause for taking a dump in the toilet.

THE MAN WHO KILLED SANTA
IN FRONT OF EVERYBODY

There aren't many people out there who can say they've gathered a crowd of children and then slain Santa Claus in front of them. But this is exactly what John McPhee managed to do in Tucson, Arizona.

During the Recession of 1958, which as the name implies was a bit of a shitter, Arizona newspaper editor John McPhee was asked by the organisers of a Christmas parade[1] if he could drum up some interest in it. With sales down, they needed a lot of people to attend and then buy Christmas presents afterwards. They were probably only hoping for a few column inches or some free advertising space, but McPhee took this request like Frodo accepting the ring. He decided to create a stunt that would have the whole town turn out to watch. He was going to have a Santa Claus jump out of a plane, right in the middle of the parade.

He hired a professional skydiver to do the task, and purchased a costume for him to use. For safety reasons, both the skydiver and McPhee decided that Santa would jump out of the plane and land in a field near the town, close enough for residents to see, before then making his way into the parade on foot.

The town was enthusiastic about the idea, and when the day came children and their parents began packing themselves into the streets to watch the one and only Santa Claus fall gracefully from the sky. McPhee went off to help prepare the skydiver transform into Santa, but it was at this point that the idea hit a snag: Santa Claus was off his tits.

McPhee found the skydiver in a local bar, far too fucked-up on drink to jump out of a plane. Even if he did make it to the ground, it was likely that the religious locals wouldn't be too pleased with him stumbling his way towards the field, having a few tactical voms, then slurring, 'Whatch doos you wans for Christma, little Timmy?' before passing out and pissing himself in his grotto. Sending the skydiver out of the plane in his current state was clearly a no-go, but McPhee had publicised the stunt so well that everyone knew about it, and there was no backing out now. One way or another, a Santa Claus was about to take a jump out of a fucking plane.

Fortunately, he had another brilliant idea. He would floor it to town, purchase a mannequin, dress it up in the red suit, and then ask the pilot to prop 'Santa' in the open plane door so that everyone could see him, before shoving it out of the plane. When the mannequin landed gently in the field, McPhee would then dash over, undress it and get into the costume, before heading to the parade.

And so it was that hundreds of children and parents, at the end of a hard year, looked up and saw Santa Claus get booted out of a plane, and plummet straight into the Earth when his parachute failed to open. From their perspective, they were about to meet their hero, but instead they witnessed his murder by some airplane cunt.

McPhee rushed to the field as the largest crowd in the parade's history[2] cried and screamed. He decided to stick to his plan and dress up in the Santa costume, before heading back into town, not really thinking about how it might now look to the children as though he'd just stripped Santa's corpse and was attempting to impersonate him not minutes after his death. He decided to tell people that surviving falls from planes was just part of Santa's magic, despite how much it would stand out amongst his other, more wholesome powers. 'Look, kids, he can fly around the world in one night, eat an unholy amount of mince pies, and can drive a fucking ice pick through his skull and feel nothing – these are just St Nick's abilities, OK?'

When he arrived in town to explain this, he found it was a ghost town. The parents and children had fled, with parents believing they too might have witnessed an actual death.

The incident would haunt McPhee for years. 'From behind closed doors you could hear the wails of heart-broken children,' he told the *Arizona Daily Star* twenty years later. 'I'm the man who "killed" Santa Claus and I'm sorry.'

THE PRANKSTER WHO COULD HAVE CAUSED A NUCLEAR MELTDOWN

Any Americans who sat and watched *Chernobyl* and sneered at the disaster caused by a fear of displeasing Soviet commanders should know this: there was once a nuclear disaster in the US that may have been caused by ass-pinching.

The SL-1 was an experimental low-power nuclear reactor in Idaho, intended to power small remote military facilities in the early 1960s. Nobody wants to have designed a device so bad it leads to new safety measures following a fucking catastrophe, but that's what this first iteration of the reactor very much was. The problem was that during maintenance, control rods – which absorb neutrons in the core of the reactor – needed to be manually pulled up just a few inches before being reconnected. Should the rods be withdrawn too far, it would be – to put it in far too lay layman's terms – boom-boom time.

And so it was that on 3 January 1961, Richard Legg, one of the operators, pulled out the rod too far, causing the SL-1 to go critical. Three people died in the boom-boom, with Legg himself being impaled through his groin by the rod, which exited through his shoulder and pinned him to the ceiling.

When you walk in on a scene like that, and your Geiger counter is going tits, you tend to wonder, 'What happened here? Richard isn't usually pinned to the ceiling and dead,' and so an investigation was ordered by the military. The investigation discovered that, prior to turning Richard into the least appetising kebab on record, the rod had been withdrawn twenty inches, rather than a few centimetres as per the instructions. It's amazing to me that we can achieve nuclear fusion, something completely unimaginable just a few centuries ago, but it can still get deadly simply by someone yanking the boom-boom stick too hard.

The investigators knew what caused the explosion, but nothing about the circumstances leading up to it. But they had a few theories, and one of them would make it the stupidest nuclear incident on record. Richard 'future kebab' Legg, it turns out, had a reputation for being a bit of a prankster – something I would argue should disqualify you from being anywhere near a fucking nuclear reactor. In my opinion, 'This guy's a bit of a wacky rascal japester' should never be answered with 'Hand him this fucking uranium'.

His pranks weren't limited to the usual fart cushion of the era, and would occasionally interfere with his work. For example, on one occasion, he had turned off a fan that was used to cool part of the reactor in order to set off the alarm on purpose,[1] the joke being, 'Haha, you all thought you were going to die horribly and never see your kids again.'

As such, there was a theory that the 1961 accident was due to 'goosing', the act of sneaking up to someone and pinching them on the bum. This theory needed testing, and in one of the oddest experiments in nuclear history, the investigators got a large group of volunteers to conduct normal operations on a replica rod. They then snuck up on them one by one and pinched them on the arse to see if it made them jump enough to feasibly make everyone in the room die. Imagine getting a degree in nuclear physics and then being forced to test the 'ass-crack bandit theory'. 'We looked at goosing,' C. Wayne Bills, one of the investigators told the author of *Idaho Falls: The Untold Story of America's First Nuclear Accident*.[2] 'You know, someone grabbing the guy on the rod in the rear and having him jump.'

The results of the experiment were, disappointingly, inconclusive. Nobody was startled enough by their goosing that they threw the rod high enough to cause a nuclear disaster, but then no other explanation seemed to fit either.

Whether Richard was the cause of the accident or not, we may never know, but his pranks definitely led to a big group of volunteers asking, 'What the fuck, I'm trying to help investigate a tragic nuclear disaster here, why are you pinching my ass?'

COMMODUS

Commodus is somehow much worse than you'd expect of a man named after a toilet. Born in 161 AD, son of Marcus Aurelius and heir to the Roman Empire, Commodus is a classic example of what happens to someone when they're too powerful to be told to fucking chill. When he took over power in 180 AD, having ruled jointly with his father for the previous four years, Commodus initially paid little attention to the matters of governing the Roman Empire and focused on his true passion: maiming small animals and demanding that people clap.

Commodus took the unusual step of taking part directly in gladiatorial combat with animals. This sounds impressive, or at least needlessly showy, until you realise precisely how little danger he was actually in. 'He descended to the arena from his place above and cut down all the domestic animals that approached him,' our old friend Cassius Dio, who witnessed the events, wrote of Commodus's gladiatorial prowess,[1] 'and some were led up to him or were brought before him in nets.'

After some light netted-kitten stabbing, Commodus would also fight larger animals such as hippos and tigers, provided they were restrained and he could pick them off from a distance with a spear. Just like in the wild. After lunch, he would 'fight' gladiators, using wooden swords, and would win every time. Part of this, you'll no doubt be shocked to hear, is likely due to gladiators not wanting to embarrass an emperor famed for his bloodlust. During the fourteen days of spectacle witnessed by Dio, for example, several gladiatorial victors refused to kill their defeated foes, resulting in Commodus binding the victors all together and making them fight to the death, like a bunch of netted kittens.

This was pretty small fry compared to his other stunts, however. On one occasion, Commodus wanted to re-enact the Sixth Labour of Hercules, in which Hercules killed some man-eating birds. He did this by shooting spectators – representing the birds – with a bow and arrow, represented by a bow and arrow. I'll level with you: he essentially shot some spectators and said, 'Hey look at me, Ma, I'm Hercules.'

On another, much worse occasion, he rounded up all the men in the city who had, for one reason or another, lost their feet, before 'fastening about their knees some likenesses of serpents' bodies, and giving them sponges to throw instead of stones' in order to defend themselves. You'll no doubt note that sponges are largely not known for their utility in combat, but for their ability to wash your balls. He then had them killed 'with blows of a club, pretending that they were giants'.[2] During all of this, he forced his senators to chant, 'Thou art lord and thou art first, of all men most fortunate. Victor thou art, and victor thou shalt be; from everlasting, Amazonian, thou art victor,' while clubbing to death what can only be described as disabled men bathing.

Irony fans will be pleased that Commodus met his own end at the hands of his wrestling partner, who strangled him to death in a bathtub.[3] This may sound a little grim, but by Commodus' own rules can be rescued by us imagining his killer yelling something about Neptune as he choked the defenceless naked bather to death while he played with his rubber duckies.

THE DOCTOR WHO THOUGHT GOAT BALLS COULD CURE EVERYTHING

I've got a grudging respect for Dr John R. Brinkley. I'll say this about the man: there aren't many people out there who can convince anyone that what they really need in their life is a third testicle, and that it should be taken from a goat. But this is exactly what Brinkley did in early twentieth-century America.

Having bought a fraudulent medical degree from the Kansas City Eclectic Medical University in 1912, like he was picking up some milk, Brinkley began earning enough money as a fake doctor to actually go to medical school and complete his course. Credit where it's due, he told the truth, just several years in advance of when it was actually true.

In 1917, he settled in the complete shithole of Milford, Kansas, which was yet to have any modern-day conveniences such as paved roads, running water, or a doctor whose solution to every problem wasn't 'I'm going to ram a third testicle in your nut sack'. For a time, though, he acted like a normal doctor, travelling around and performing minor surgeries for cash. Then one day he had a bizarre encounter with an old man that completely changed his course.

The old man, who was a meatpacker, came into his office for a chat, and apparently talked for quite some time about other topics before he stopped beating about the bush and told Brinkley he was impotent. Quite why he felt it was better to have a long chat about life before getting to the 'My meat isn't packing' portion of the conversation is unclear, but to each their own. The man asked Brinkley to do what he could to fix his problem, but Brinkley insisted that not much could be done. Brinkley, likely trying to lighten the mood, made a joke about how the old man wouldn't have this trouble if he had the testicles of one of the goats at the old meatpacking plant.[1] A little pointer: if you go to your doctor about your testicles and they tell you 'What you need are some goat balls', you are well within your rights to ask to see a different GP.

Here's where things took a turn. The old man began to insist that the doctor put the goat testicles in him. Despite Brinkley's protests of 'What if someone hears you have a goat testicle?' and 'Also you might die', Brinkley eventually decided to do the operation. If, to you, this sounds like just the kind of reluctance a conman would feign in order to get their mark more interested, congratulations: you would not have fallen for the old three-testicle switcharoo, as the professionals surely call it.

A date was set, and the old man brought a goat around to the office in the dead of night, which to be honest seems more nefarious than were he simply to admit to the whole town 'GETTING MYSELF A GOAT PLUM, NOTHING TO WORRY ABOUT. JUST GETTING ONE OF HIS KNACKERS PUT INTO MY KNACKERS'.

The operation was . . . I don't want to say 'a success' here, but the old man definitely left with one more testicle in his scrotum than he had previously. Post-op, the man had to have a cover story for why he was laid up in bed – one that didn't involve a goat. As such, whenever he needed his new testicle checking, he would ring and say to Brinkley that he had the flu and needed a visit, cleverly not mentioning 'I'm pleased with my new testicle', in case an operator was listening in on the call.

Word did get around, however, and before long a surprising number of impotent men (desperate as they were) asked him to perform the operation, despite the side effects – the main one being that the men's scrotums began to reek of goat meat. Men did report that they got their mojo (full erections) back, but you can sure as hell put this down to a placebo effect: though Brinkley said he was attaching the new testicle to blood vessels within the balls, he was in fact merely cutting open the sack and plonking it in there beneath the skin.[2]

Following an advertising scheme selling the goat operation as a miracle cure, Brinkley came into a lot of money and used it to build a hospital in the town, complete with an area to raise goats.

His reputation grew, and he decided that the goat testicle no longer just cured impotence, but was good for a range of other conditions. Schizophrenia? Whack a testicle in there. Dementia? Testicle. Flatulence? Going to shock you here and say pop a ball in.

As much as I'd like to call Brinkley a complete asshole (he was charging $750 per operation for a cure that essentially just gave your balls something to clack against) he did use some of the money he made to enrich the town around him, paying to install electricity in the town, as well as a sewerage system.

His operation expanded, and he set up a legally dubious radio station down in Mexico, primarily to push a whole line of 'cures' using goat balls, earning himself enough to own a ridiculously large mansion with a giant collection of Cadillacs. But, as the old saying goes, you can't keep opening up old men's scrotums and putting goat bollocks in there without breaking a few old men. Before he could die rich, he was up to his own balls in malpractice suits, after quite a number of patient deaths via infection.[3] He died penniless, awaiting trial for an unrelated mail fraud. Say what you will about the man, he had one hell of a work ethic.

ELIZABETH BÁTHORY/ELIZABETH BÁTHORY'S ACCUSERS, DEPENDING ON YOUR PERSPECTIVE

There are two versions of the story of Elizabeth Báthory, and thankfully for the premise of this book, they are both full to the brim with human anuses. In both versions, she was born in 1560 as a Hungarian noblewoman to the wealthy Báthory family. In 1573, she married Count Ferenc Nádasdy and had several children with him. Nádasdy became chief commander of the Hungarian army, leaving Elizabeth in charge of their homes, lands and local government.[1]

Then, depending on who's telling the story, she either doesn't start torturing and bathing in the blood of her servants, or she does, before she is bricked into her room to die.

The version you might know

While Nádasdy was away with the army, rumours began circulating that something not right was going on in the Báthory castle – and by 'not right' I of course mean several brutal murders, dismemberments and slatherings in honey, followed shortly by feedings to bugs.

Years later, after Nádasdy's death in 1604, Hungarian King Matthias II sent György Thurzó – Elizabeth's own cousin[2] – to investigate the rumours. He found three hundred witnesses that were willing to swear that Báthory had a hobby of luring local peasant girls to the castle with promises of giving them work as her servant. She would then spend her time brutally beating them, freezing them, burning them, jamming needles or scissors into a wide variety of their body parts, as well as biting off and eating their faces, limbs and boobs. She would also cut off various appendages, including our old friends the genitals, and beat victims to death with clubs.

According to later legends, she also took a lot of baths in the blood of virgins in an attempt to keep her youth, granting her more time to do all of the above. On this point you may be wondering, 'What the hell?' Well, she supposedly noticed by pure chance that where she had accidentally splattered the blood of her servants against her skin (something I'm sure you'll agree happens constantly), the skin appeared more youthful than the skin outside of the splash zone.

According to the investigation, Báthory, with the aid of her favourite servants to lighten the workload, ended up killing eighty girls. However, one witness claimed that they had seen Elizabeth's notes, in which she had detailed more than 650 victims. Surely the classic evil villain mistake of detailing all her crimes in one easily accessible document was enough to make people think she was a serial killer. However, to give you a sense of the reliability of witnesses in the case, another claimed to have seen her shagging Satan.

The story that's obviously true

Look, I'm the first person to assume that incredibly wealthy people are doing heinous shit in castles, but when someone starts saying 'Also Satan was there and he is a shagger', that's got to set off your Spidey-sense. The idea of her bathing in the blood of her victims was almost certainly an invention, coming as it did over a hundred years after her death.[3]

In reality, powerful families involved in Elizabeth's trial had a lot to gain from the trashing of the Báthory reputation.[4] King Matthias II owed money to Elizabeth's husband, which he wouldn't owe any more if, e.g., she too were dead. Witnesses to Báthory's crimes were also likely examined under torture, perhaps explaining why testimony was so different depending on who was asked.

The rumours, however, did not spring from nowhere. As was customary for nobles of the time, Báthory provided a small amount of healthcare to people in the area. Not being from around those parts, it's likely she brought with her practices such as bloodletting, something that to common folk may have seemed weird, and her healers – with their strange practices – were easily blamed when someone who came for help died. To be fair, when you're draining people of their blood in an attempt to help them, it's probably enough to make people think, 'Huh, maybe she is fucking Satan.'

The aftermath
Whether she was actually killing servants (no) or merely framed by a king and others who wanted her out of the picture (definitely this one), the end result was that her alleged co-murderers were executed, while she was bricked into her bedroom and fed through a little slot for the next four years until her death. What's worse is that they fed her people-food, rather than the ripped-up pieces of human flesh to which she was *definitely* unaccustomed.

THE FIRST PEOPLE TO CONDUCT BIOLOGICAL WARFARE

There are many dignified ways your remains can be dealt with after you die. A nice burial, for instance, or having your disease-ridden remains catapulted at your enemies. This latter method of saying goodbye to your loved ones has, admittedly, gone a little out of fashion (though I vote we bring it back: what makes for a more memorable funeral than launching Grandma at Grandma's foes?), but it had a brief heyday in 1346 warfare thanks to the assholes that were the Tatar-Mongols.

A dispute between the Genoese and the Tatar-Mongols for the Black Sea city of Caffa had been going on for some time, though I probably didn't need to specify that. After all, you don't go from there being no dispute to flinging your dead at a city at the first sign of a quibble. The city had around sixteen thousand citizens,[1] and was an important spot for trade in Eastern Europe in what is now Ukraine. As with a lot of disputes in the past, it came down to one side saying 'This is mine' and the other saying 'I want that'.

During one of several sieges of the city by the Tatar-Mongols, their army began to fall sick with the plague. It spread quickly amongst the men and – according to contemporary, though second-hand, source Gabriele de' Mussi – it started killing them in their thousands every day. Realising that they were, in fact, fucked, the army abandoned hope of the siege succeeding and instead focused on giving their fallen comrades a real Looney Tunes send-off.

'They ordered corpses to be placed in catapults and lobbed into the city in the hope that the intolerable stench would kill everyone inside,' a translation of the account by de' Mussi read.[2] 'What seemed like mountains of dead were thrown into the city, and the Christians could not hide or flee or escape from them, although they dumped as many of the bodies as they could in the sea.'

According to the account, those that weren't killed by the plague were inclined to flee the city (and thus spread it elsewhere) because of the overwhelming stench. Not the main point here, but you've no idea what an active downpour of rotting human flesh will do to house prices, with even the savviest of estate agents unable to convince buyers it's, at least, 'free meat'.

JAMES 'DR SHITS' MORRISON

James Morrison – remember that name by the way, because that's who I'll be referring to as Dr Shits from here on out – was a nineteenth-century doctor who thought he could cure just about everything by making people have unstoppable diarrhoea.

Dr Shits had the idea that all diseases were caused by the impurity of the blood (an idea way out of step during a time when it was believed that disease was caused by bad smells), for which the solution was profuse defecation. His initial belief came from the fact that he was able to cure his own life-long constipation[1] by creating his own laxatives. He somehow managed to extrapolate from this that making people shit better would cure things like aneurisms and smallpox.

With no further testing conducted than an 'I reckon', he created his own brand of tablets to help people crap out the bad juju. Universal Vegetable Pills were marketed by Dr Shits as being able to cure everything. One advert, for instance, showed a man who no longer needed his crutches, having shat out his bad legs.

Dr Shits, you'll be shocked to learn, wasn't too fussed about figuring out things like dosage. As far as he was concerned, if you fancied ramming down dozens of his pills, that was fine. He even recommended that you take the laxatives for the shits, 'so as to effectively carry off the morbid humours'.[2] Needless to say, this is like someone trying to treat a man's ball pain with successive blows to the testicles.

Dr Shits advised that you were likely to feel worse before you got better, and to not let that stop you from taking the very profitable medicine. The first step of healing patients, he apparently believed, was always to increase profit margins. Of course, the pills began to kill people,[3] including a little apprentice boy and a fifteen-year-old girl who died 'in horrible distress'[4] as a consequence of taking his medicine.

Dr Shits miraculously managed to avoid the blame for the deaths that kept occurring, with lower-down drug vendors being jailed for manslaughter instead. In 1836, one agent was jailed for manslaughter after a thirty-two-year-old man, who was suffering from mild knee pain,[5] was given a thousand pills over twenty days, and subsequently shat himself to death. Accusations of manslaughter kept rolling in, but Dr Shits always managed to escape scot free.

With the deaths piling up, other medical professionals began to see through the quack and started campaigning against him, but they were fairly ineffective at slowing down his sales. This may be because the adverts tended to depict people being turned into vegetation by the vegetable pills (a thing that can't happen), rather than simply telling people 'These pills will make you shit yourself to death' in large font.

Morrison eventually died in 1840, before his sons took over the business.[6] He'd earned around £5,000, around £16 million in today's money, all for the batshit claim that diarrhoea will cure diarrhoea.

CLEVER HANS THE HORSE

Look, nobody wants to be the person going around shouting 'This puppy is a dickhead' or 'That bunny is a wanker', so trust me when I say I've thought long and hard about this, and despite my best wishes, Hans the horse was an absolute asshole.

In 1900, a German mathematician named Wilhem von Osten, who was clearly having some sort of prolonged breakdown, began teaching maths to his four-year-old horse, Hans. By 1904, the maths horse was ready to take on the world.[1]

The turn of the twentieth century was a strange time, when you could say 'My horse does maths' and nobody would tell you to fuck off. In fact, people gathered in large audiences for his performances, where the horse would show that it could count, knew what date it was, could read a clock and could recognise playing cards. If you asked it for some basic sums, it could also give you the correct answer.

Probably sensing that saying the numbers out loud would be 'freaky as balls', the horse sensibly opted to tap out the answer with its hooves. Naturally, however, the people who weren't sitting around clapping and squealing at the maths horse were sceptical. If a horse was this intelligent, it raised the possibility that all horses had this potential or were just as intelligent, and that for hundreds of years humans had been riding around on something that was basically Carol Vorderman.

Then the horse really started taking the piss. After the trainer replaced numbers with letters (A=1, B=2 etc.) the horse began to tap out sentences. While most animals would look at a painting and see only potential food or a place to shit, Hans could identify the name of the painter, showing an ability to distinguish art styles. While other horses ran around getting spooked by cows or their own shadows, this cunt was tapping out 'I think you'll notice from the trademark brushstrokes that this baroque scene is a Rembrandt.'

Sceptics, of course, believed that the trainer could be signalling the answer to Hans in some way, helping it out with its horse scam, and decided to put the horse to the test. For a year and a half, a commission set up by the German Board of Education took Hans through rigorous tests to find out if he really could do all the things he seemed to be doing. The trainer was kept away for many of the tests, to eliminate the possibility that he was handing out clues.

However, no matter who asked the question, Hans the horse kept on bashing out correct answers, like a fucking dork. The commission concluded that the horse's talent was no hoax. This was a horse that could do maths, and name composers from sound alone, without any formal classical education.

They never suspected that it was the horse who was doing the con. After the commission failed to find any cheating, a better investigator got involved. In 1907, biologist and psychologist Professor Oscar Pfungst took on the horse and figured out its trick. He found that when the questioner knew the answer to what they were asking, the horse would return the right answer. If the questioner had no clue what the answer was, the horse would stare at you like, well, a horse, before returning the wrong number of hoof taps.

He realised that the asshole horse hadn't been putting the work in, but had merely been noticing the reactions on the questioner's face. When Hans had tapped out the correct number, he noticed the tension on their face relax, and knew to stop tapping, convincing everyone from idiots to idiots with degrees that he was some kind of genius.

Following the revelation, the crowds understandably turned on the horse. This wasn't a maths horse, it was merely a horse that could read complex emotional facial cues on a wide variety of people's faces and then respond accordingly, and therefore worthless glue.

The con horse quickly fell out of favour now that people knew the truth, and it was lost track of. From what we know, Hans was drafted into the First World War, and either killed in action or eaten by hungry soldiers. A fitting end for an asshole horse.

VICTORIANO ÁLVAREZ

There were few things people enjoyed more in the early twentieth century than dying in a pointless war and islands covered in shit. Combining these two interests is the story of murderous lighthouse keeper Victoriano Álvarez and Clipperton Island.

Back in 1528, a small uninhabited island was discovered by Spaniard Alvaro Saavedra Cerón, a thousand kilometres off the coast of Mexico. Clipperton Island, as it would eventually become known, was dank, crab-infested, and – to the delight of just about everyone – completely covered in shit. The poo – guano – belonged to bats and seabirds, was crammed full of nitrogen, and so was perfect for restoring nutrients to soil.

Naturally, several countries tried to stake a claim to the island over the centuries, even if it was thousands of miles from their own land, including the US, Britain and France. In the beginning of the twentieth century, Mexico laid its own claim to the guano-rich Clipperton Island, and sent settlers and soldiers. In 1914, America withdrew its presence, fearing the dangers of the island's severe weather were not worth the sweet, sweet bird shit that they could scoop up there. The Mexican inhabitants were advised by the Americans to flee too,[1] but now that they had control of the island, they weren't so easily persuaded.

About twenty-six people now lived on the island. Had they been born late enough to realise that this was roughly the same size as the cast of *Lost*, perhaps alarm bells would have gone off. But these poor chumps hadn't even read *Lord of the Flies*, and so weren't aware of the importance of a big conch and bullying some kid named Piggy to pass the time. And so the thirteen soldiers, twelve women and children, and a lone lighthouse keeper – Victoriano Álvarez, who kept to himself – settled down to collect the guano, with only occasional visits from Mexican supply ships to break the isolation.

Then, one day in 1917, the ships stopped coming. With revolution happening in Mexico, the government sort of forgot about the island and its inhabitants, and left them to their own devices. Unfortunately, these devices were zero information from the outside world and profound vitamin deficiency. For a short time, the inhabitants – led by a man named Ramón Arnaud – survived on fish, eggs, the seabirds the eggs popped out of, and the occasional coconut to take the taste away.

An American ship attempted to rescue the islanders, but Arnaud decided not to abandon the post[2] and risk others laying claim to the island, instead choosing to remain and work on developing some hardcore scurvy. The islanders grew malnourished, weak, and quite often dead. The bodies were buried deep in the sand to protect them from the crabs. Then one day, when Arnaud believed he had spotted a ship (he hadn't), he made the situation far worse by asking three of the healthier soldiers left to join him in rowing out to greet it, before promptly drowning. Family members who watched from the shore believed that the soldiers, upon realising that there was no ship, attempted to wrestle Arnaud's weapon from him before they all fell overboard.

A few hours later, a hurricane hit the island, and the remaining women and children hid in a basement, while Arnaud's widow Alicia Rovira gave birth. Probably muttering 'Well, I don't see how this situation could get any worse', they emerged to find that Victoriano Álvarez had taken the opportunity to gather up all the weapons on the island bar his own, hurl them into the sea, and to then start proclaiming himself king of the island.

The next few years were hell. Alvarez, perhaps driven to insanity by the lonely life of a lighthouse keeper, or maybe driven to becoming a lighthouse keeper by virtue of being an asshole who knew he should be kept away from anything more sentient than a lightbulb, was a ruthless dictator to his new 'subjects'. He raped the remaining women and children, and murdered those he found to be uncooperative. He moved his way through the women, getting bored with his victims and switching to another on a regular basis.

With no hope of rescue, no way of getting off the island and no weapons, the islanders were stuck with Álvarez and his brutal beatings until 1917, when he turned his attention to Alicia Rovira Arnaud, demanding that she come to the lighthouse one morning. Arnaud arrived with fellow islander Tirza Randon, who ran inside what I suppose was the island's shit-covered equivalent of a palace, and returned with a hammer. She struck Álvarez on the back of the head twice, while Arnaud found an axe and joined the party. After likely killing him with the axe, she stabbed the body repeatedly with a knife to make sure, before using the blade to slash at his face. If, somehow, you feel bad for Álvarez, you should know that at this point, Arnaud was one of the only three surviving women on the island, the others having died at his hands.

Timing, it seems, was not the islanders' strong point. While stood there over a fresh corpse covered in stab wounds and holding a big knife, axe, hammer, and now their tormenter's rifle, probably looking a bit murdery, they glanced up at the horizon and saw a ship. The USS *Yorktown* saw the gathered islanders, and attempted to send a small boat to rescue the three remaining women and their children.

When the first boat was unable to get close (hey, there's a reason they had a lighthouse keeper, even if they didn't have a very good lighthouse-keeper-hiring process) the women discussed suicide. Just as they were deciding whether or not to drown or shoot themselves, the *Yorktown* sent out a second boat, which made it to the island. At last, the women and children were rescued.

The crew onboard the ship, to their credit, kept the murder and circumstances a secret for a full seventeen years, in order to protect the women from any legal consequences of murdering their tormentor. Sort of like a much more gritty Sawyer from *Lost*.

KING EDWARD III

The Black Death was – and I don't want to be controversial here – somewhat of a shitter. There aren't many bright sides to 60 per cent of Europe's population being wiped out in just a few years, unless you happen to be a funeral director who specialises in bulk deals. However, if you were one of the lucky ones who survived, there was sort of an upside to millions of your fellow workers dying of a horrible disease. As well as less competition for the microwave, you faced less competition at work, and could use this to your advantage in wage negotiations, which at the time would have gone something like this:

'I'd like to be paid double.'

'No.'

'OK, fine. Come back to me if Dead Bob refuses to do it on the cheap.'

People who had survived the plague, however, were shit out of luck when it came to wage negotiation, thanks to a Statute of Labourers brought in by King Edward III in 1351. The statute essentially compelled workers to pretend like the last five years had never happened. While that might be appealing to people who e.g. wanted their wife Carol not to be dead, the law was in fact a lot more limited in scope, forcing wage labourers to accept wages that they would have been paid back in 1346. What's more, the statute also prevented able-bodied people from saying 'fuck that' (or 'verily, fuck that' if we're going to be authentic) by requiring 'that every person, able in body and under the age of sixty years, not having enough to live upon, being required, shall be bound to serve him that doth require him, or else be committed to gaol until he shall find surety to serve'.[1] That is, if you can work, you will be forced to work for a pittance if you want to avoid being thrown in jail with the nonces on E Wing.

Once a person had served their gaol time, they would be back on the market, forced to work for pre-plague wages. The law was also particularly tough on anyone who had looked at these goings-on and thought, 'Maybe I'll do something better with my life than medieval serfdom,' and fancied a change of career. 'If a reaper or mower, or other workman or servant, of whatever standing or condition he be, who is retained in the service of any one, do depart from the said service before the end of the term agreed, without permission or reasonable cause, he shall undergo the penalty of imprisonment,' the decree stated.[2]

The idea was, of course, to drive down inflation, keeping prices from escalating through imposed wages – i.e. by taking quite a large piss on the poorest in society, who, I really must stress, had spent the last five years listening to their friends and family say 'Does this bubo look a bit red to you?', shortly before starting funeral arrangements (a.k.a. finding a big hole already filled with piles of your friends).

The laws were mainly enforced against peasants rather than employers, who got all the benefits of being able to revert wages from a pittance (wages before the plague hit were already low, having been hit hard by a recession) to a pre-plague double pittance without the stress of themselves being paid less.

Though the laws were hard to enforce, the statute technically remained in place until 1444, pretty much making all labourers wish they'd had the good sense to just fucking die of the plague when they had the chance.

THE US AND THEIR RIDICULOUS PLAN TO NUKE THE MOON

'One small step for man, one giant leap for mankind.' Those were the famous words heard when humans first landed on the Moon. If Project A119 had gone ahead, however, we would have heard something a little more like 'Kerpoooooowowowowoowwwww' followed by the unmistakable sound of a nuclear fucking winter.

The US were famously not very chill about the space race. Having been beaten into space by the Soviet Union, they were desperate to catch up and overtake their communist counterparts. Project A119[1] – a title so dull it was probably kept secret by people assuming it was about reconstruction of an A road – sought to show the Soviets who was boss, by nuking the goddamn Moon. 'The Air Force wanted a mushroom cloud so large it would be visible on Earth,' Dr Leonard Reiffel, who led the project back in 1959, told the *Observer* in 2000. 'The theory was that if the bomb exploded on the edge of the moon, the mushroom cloud would be illuminated by the sun.'[2]

The Moon, sat up there minding its own business, was also at risk from a similar project by the Soviet Union. Having done nothing but control the tides, scare the shit out of medieval peasants by making the sun go away, and make life on Earth possible in the first place, it now faced a nuclear threat from both sides of the Cold War. As the old saying goes, my enemy's enemy is apparently the fucking Moon.

Funnily enough, there were many reasons why nuking the Moon was such a terrible idea. One major problem is that destroying the lunar surface would make it much more difficult to study in the future. There were also other smaller problems such as nuclear fallout, which would make it dangerous for colonies to be set up there. I know setting up colonies on the Moon seems unlikely now anyway, but this was a time when they thought the 1980s would play out like *The Jetsons*. Another potential hazard was: what if they missed, and the missile ended up returning to Earth? Not the main thing here, but it would be embarrassing if aliens found us centuries from now and discovered we'd boomeranged ourselves into extinction.

In the end, the project was cancelled, but not because everyone took a step back and realised how absurd it would be to nuke the Moon just to make the Soviets look like chumps and potentially provoke a nuclear space race, but because they concluded that they could accidentally end up nuking Earth while trying to get the weapon out of the atmosphere. Instead they ended up sending pretty much the opposite thing on the deadly spectrum: a grown man who went by the name of Neil.

Occasionally, when I am at my lowest ebb and wondering if humanity will survive, I remember that we once looked up in wonder at the night sky and thought, 'Imma nuke the shit out of that Moon,' and it comforts me to know that we now definitely won't.

HERMAN SÖRGEL

In the 1920s, German architect Herman Sörgel came up with an idea for solving all of Europe's problems, chief of which was that the place had tended to be a bit war-y of late. He, like many others at the time, thought that there wasn't much that couldn't be solved with a good old-fashioned land grab. His plans, however, were less traditional than trying to take it with a big gun, as had been done by so many in the past.

Sörgel wanted to drain the Mediterranean Sea. The idea, named Atlantropa, which he dedicated his whole life to, was to create three gigantic dams that would block off the sea from the ocean, creating a new landmass that connected Europe with Africa,[1] and generating enough power for the entirety of Europe at the same time. I realise he had the disadvantage of being born before James Bond, but that's no excuse for his not reading the plan aloud to himself and exclaiming, 'Fuck me I've gone a bit Bond villain here,' and rededicating his life to something less patently evil.

Atlantropa as a concept was a lot less murdery than other ideas soon to be floated, what with Sörgel being a pacifist. Hell, it was even eco-friendly. It's just that it happened to be incredibly, horribly racist. How racist, you ask? Well, he ended up pitching it to the Nazis. Picture *Dragons' Den* but instead of Deborah Meaden it's Adolf Hitler.

You see, Atlantropa – which gained a surprising number of supporters, and for a time was taken relatively seriously – was all about improving things for Europeans, with little regard paid to the continent of Africa. Imagine a neighbour smashed down your wall, joined their house to your house, then proudly announced, 'Things will be greatly improved for me in this new superhouse, which will henceforth be known as my house,' and you'll have a rough idea of the sort of vibe Sörgel was going for.

The continent of Africa was to be used by Europeans,[2] with Africans there only as labourers. I'd therefore argue that it was a bit much of Herman to describe himself as a pacifist, when part of his plan was to dam the Congo River and flood much of central Africa, with no regard for the people who relied on, well, not being drowned by a mad fucking architect to live. It also isn't much of a testament to what you're like as a person when you adapt your idea to make it more appealing to the Nazis[3] before pitching it to them directly, both of which Herman did.

Despite ticking a lot of the racist boxes, which the Nazis loved, they were too busy trying to fight the Soviets to take Sörgel up on his idea, and so he didn't manage to secure his investment. Having failed to convince even some of the most evil people on the planet of his supervillain plan, you'd think he would give up – but you'd be wrong.

I'd imagine the psychology of the situation was pretty much this: Sörgel probably thought to himself, 'If I drop the idea of creating a giant supercontinent now, that means that for the last twenty years I have been doing something that is verifiably quite fucking unhinged.' So rather than drop his plans, he continued to push for the project, and refused to even modify the racist elements where he planned to just flood a highly populated region of Africa because he wanted a lake, or to use the new supercontinent for the benefit of only the Europeans.

He ended up dying in 1952 after being run over on his way to deliver a speech on Atlantropa in Munich, having spent his life showing commitment to a truly terrible idea, the likes of which would never be seen again until *Game of Thrones* season 8.

HANNAH DUSTON AND THE SCALP-HUNGRY COLONISERS

In the seventeenth century, American colonisers made a hero out of a woman who got herself a big handful of scalps.

Born in Haverhill, Massachusetts in 1657, Hannah Duston got caught up in a war between the Native American Abenaki peoples allied with the French (who wanted to stop the expansion of the English colonies) and the English colonists of New England (who wanted to spread like Covid-19, or some other worse disease that makes you shit yourself to death).

The Abenaki peoples regularly conducted raids on English colonies, and on 15 March 1697 Hannah Duston was captured, along with several of her neighbours, before being taken on their way north to Canada where the raiders were based. Early on in the journey, Duston's newborn baby was killed by her captors.[1]

After a couple of weeks, Duston and her neighbour Mary Neff were housed with a Native American family, along with a fourteen-year-old boy – Samuel Leonardson – who had been captured a year before. Leonardson got on well with his captors, and had possibly even been adopted, which Duston used to her own advantage. She asked Leonardson to ask one of the captors to explain the best way to kill someone with a tomahawk. He did, which, to be fair, should have raised a few red flags, what with all the tomahawks lying around the place. The Native American man he asked obliged, explaining the complex process of hitting them hard with the pointy bit. If you need more details than that, I highly recommend you a) calm down, and b) please google it so that the FBI can put you on a list.

While the captor family/hosts were sleeping, Duston, Neff and Leonardson – who, though he got on well with his captors, had still, nonetheless, been kidnapped – grabbed themselves some tomahawks and set about murdering pretty much the entire family as they slept. The trio killed ten of the family, six of whom were children, more than evening out the dead-kid score against a family which had not captured her nor killed her kid. 'Ah, but she wanted vengeance on the enemy,' I hear you think, to which I refer you to point a) in the previous paragraph.

The three managed to escape via canoe, but before they did so they took the time to scalp the whole family, including the six children, to which you might reasonably respond, 'What the fuck?' Well, contrary to 1950s American films that depict Native Americans as savages who scalped their victims, it transpires that colonists were much more into this below-the-hairline mandatory haircut than they are in the movies. See, the English, after arriving in America and looking at the people who already lived there, probably thought, 'That won't do,' in the way the English tend to before embarking on some atrocities. It's therefore likely the English decided to use the practice of scalping against the Native Americans too.[2]

Various tribes had likely already been scalping victims since before colonial times, just as Europeans had for centuries. So when the English saw Native Americans do it, they thought they could get in on the action and kill a few birds with one big horrible knife: they could pay bounty hunters in return for the scalps, and they could get their revenge on the Native Americans.

Bounty hunters, who are not exactly known for their loyalty to the honour system, were asked by English colonialists to kill Native Americans for money. Rather than demand they bring in a whole body, or even just the head, the colonialists realised they could save a lot of weight ferrying the bodies to and fro if they only asked for the scalp. Treating their enemy with very little respect (it's not like, following her funeral, you would be fine with the funeral director burying 'a bit' of Grandma), they started paying £50 sterling for female and child Native Americans, or double that for males aged twelve and above.[3] The high price for the scalps led to bounty hunters going on sprees, as well as taking the scalps of colonists and passing them off as Native Americans,[4] something that's much easier to do when you're only presenting a small portion of the head. In terms of household chores, it's like being asked whether you've done the dishes and handing over an admittedly quite clean teaspoon as incontrovertible proof.

And so it was that Hannah Duston scalped her child victims for the money. For centuries afterwards, and in the statue that was eventually created of her showing her carrying a handful of scalps, she was portrayed as a hero for her scalp-frenzy, while Native Americans got judged as savages for exactly the same grim act. If they were really being fair, at best the colonisers could have remarked, 'That's barbaric,' before adding, 'They aren't even getting paid.'

THE GREEK MYSTIC WITH AN IMPRESSIVE COMMAND OF SOCK PUPPETS

Alexander of Abonoteichus was born in Greece around 105 AD, at a time when you could shove your hand up a snake puppet and have people worship it as a god – which, as his later life involved a lot of this, was pretty fortunate for old Alexander.

The main source of information on Alexander is his contemporary Lucian of Samosata, a man who, by his own account, thought Alex 'a person whose deserts entitled him not to be read about by the cultivated, but to be torn to pieces in the amphitheatre by apes or foxes, with a vast audience looking on'.[1] Imagine having the only remaining tales of your life come from an enemy who has sat down and decided which specific animals you deserve to be torn to shreds by for entertainment purposes.

Lucian tells the story of Alexander in a letter about ten years after his death, after making it perfectly clear that he thought the person asking about Alexander was a dick for doing so: 'I confess to being a little ashamed both on your account and my own. There are you asking that the memory of an arch-scoundrel should be perpetuated in writing.' He then, grudgingly, admits that Alexander was an attractive and charismatic youth, which helped him to con people later on.[2] Alexander fell in with a man called Cocconas, who Lucian believed to be 'a man of still worse character' than Alexander. The name Cocconas refers to pomegranate seeds, and may be a reference to testicles. Alexander was essentially such a shithead that he teamed up with a man calling himself 'Knackers'. The two formed a double act as occultists, pretending to have magical powers for money, sort of like a Penn and Teller dedicated to evil. They went around 'shearing "fatheads"',[3] which essentially meant conning the ignorant and unnecessarily stupid out of their money.

The pair, according to Lucian, decided on a bigger con: they would pretend that Alexander was Asclepius, a god of medicine and son of Apollo, a feat so bold it makes George Clooney switching briefcases in order to get some cash in *Ocean's 11* look like pure dogshit. The pair buried a stone tablet in the temple of Apollo, which detailed that Asclepius and his dad were about to show up reincarnated in Pontus, before allowing that tablet to be discovered a few days later.

While Knackers died from a snake bite and took an early exit from this tale, Alexander grew his hair and tried to look significantly more prophety. He began to pretend he was insane, and forced himself to foam at the mouth by eating soap – a sight that, today, would prompt the question 'Why is that man eating soap?' rather than taking him seriously as a Jesus.

It was here where things got puppety.

'The two had long ago manufactured and fitted up a serpent's head of linen; they had given it a more or less human expression, and painted it very like the real article,' Lucian wrote. 'By a contrivance of horsehair, the mouth could be opened and shut, and a forked black serpent tongue protruded, working on the same system.'[4]

Essentially, they had stuck some eyes on a sock, and Alexander was about to make people worship it. First, he took a reptile and placed it into an empty goose egg, carefully repaired with wax, before hiding it. Next, he stood in the middle of the marketplace, naked but for a gold-spangled loin cloth, and started yelling at everybody just attempting to buy, for example, some cress. He told them, by way of chanting, that Asclepius was about to show up, before leading them to the egg and cracking it open in front of them. Having pretty low thresholds in terms of burdens of proof (look, I don't want to be that guy, but maybe Lucian had a point when he called them fatheads), when the egg cracked open and a lizard popped out, this was apparently proof enough for the locals that they were in the presence of Asclepius himself, rather than some sort of egg mishap.

With the hard bit out of the way, Alexander now moved on to the next part of the con: finding a big room with shit lighting. His venue requirements were simple: it had to be able to fit a bunch of fatheads and have so little light that people couldn't tell the difference between a sock puppet and an actual god. When he'd settled on an appropriate place, and with a crowd now forming, he took out his puppet and made it talk, declaring its name to be Glycon, and claiming that Zeus was its grandad – presumably after Zeus fucked Big Bird or one of the Muppets.

Using a few magic tricks, such as opening letters from the audience containing questions and resealing them when he had read the contents, he was able to convince throngs of people – whose heads may have been of the fat variety – that the puppet was a god. The god then started telling the future, and in return was given gifts by crowds of people, none of whom thought to bring some less shitty lighting.

Over time, Glycon's fame spread, and – according to Lucian – it was taken seriously by the emperor Marcus Aurelius. Marcus – again, with a big 'ACCORDING TO LUCIAN' klaxon here – sought the puppet's advice on battle, and was told that victory had been foreseen. He took the puppet at its word, and shortly thereafter suffered a massive defeat at the hands of enemies who hadn't acted on the strategic military advice of a sock.

THE SEX CULT THAT TRIED TO TAKE OVER OREGON

In the 1980s, the members of a hippy commune/sex cult – the Rajneesh movement – carried out the biggest biological attack in US history. The cult, which preached open attitudes towards sex and sex therapies, launched the attack in an attempt to take control of Oregon.

In the 1960s, mystic Bhagwan Shree Rajneesh founded the cult while travelling throughout India. There was farming, there were 'people having orgasmic sex all the time. All night, like mating baboons, gibbons.'[1]

After pressure from the Indian government to stop, and to also pay their goddamn tax, the cult soon fled and set up shop in a ranch in Oregon, where Rajneesh had once gone for medical attention, taking over seven thousand followers with them.[2] The commune grew quickly, and even had its own airfield, should you ever want to take a plane ride and admire the scale of the orgy barns. For a time, the cult's members lived in peaceful bliss, by which I of course mean a lot of them were off their tits and their children were allowed to run wild, unburdened by parental guidance or anyone following child labour laws.

But it wasn't long before things took a turn for the worse. A number of factors led to the cult carrying out some pretty questionable activities such as rounding up homeless people, conducting a massive wiretap operation, murder attempts, and plans to make the whole county shit themselves via a biological attack.

The first problem was that Rajneesh hadn't read the lease properly before he bought the ranch, and didn't realise that he would need quite a lot of planning permission to expand. The second was that he had taken a four-year vow of silence, leaving the actual running of the cult to a much more ruthless character, Sheela Patel, who would stop at nothing to continue to grow it.

The cult would need to win over the local government or get its own candidates into power if it was to be allowed to expand its operation. A third problem was that Sheela Patel was a fairly disagreeable asshole. When attempting to bribe a local environmental group failed,[3] her tactics turned more ruthless. Through sheer numbers, the cult was able to take over an election in the local town of Antelope, overthrowing its leaders and changing the name of the town to Rajneesh.

As well as being at odds with the community it had overtaken, the cult was objectively annoying. For example, during an Antelope town council meeting, it renamed a recycling centre 'The Adolf Hitler Recycling Center'.[4] As a result of the coup, the cult had gained a lot of powers, including one that allowed the sex cult to have its own police force, which seems like an awful lot of effort to put into what was essentially a slave-run sex club with a silent host, but I'm not here to judge. But the Wasco County Commission – responsible for matters of town planning – continued to hamper the cult's expansion, and so the cult plotted to take it over.

With several seats coming up in the commission election, the initial plan was some classic voter fraud. They would ship in homeless people from around the US, offering them a place to stay in return for their vote come election day. However, the commission soon became aware of this and changed the rules of the election so that you would have to prove at least twenty days' residency before being able to vote. Rather than pull off a coup, the cult had merely washed a lot of homeless people. Which was nice, but not very on brand.

Next, the cult – and remember, this was all in between their main project of banging each other around the clock – planned the assassination of the Oregon District Attorney, Charles Taylor. The plan was aborted, likely for being horrific and/or a logistical nightmare. However, a plan that they did go through with was to make everyone shit their guts out, be they county commissioner or a lowly voter.

Now, should you ever feel the urge to make yourself a poison lab, I would argue that that would be a great point to take stock and really think about your lifestyle. But, anyway, the cult built a poison lab, and here the crew shipped in poisons and bacteria such as typhoid to test and replicate, ready to hit the public with. Having already decided against pulverising some beavers and then leaving their rotten flesh upstream in order to infect voters, they opted to hit the town with salmonella. The idea was simple: people who are shitting water are unlikely to think, 'You know what, I really feel like voting right now,' leaving the cult members free to overwhelm the polls.

To test this very complex system (feed someone something that makes them shit themselves then wait for them to shit themselves), they poisoned a Wasco County official who came to visit the ranch, before having a (quite wet) dry run at poisoning the public. In the practice attack, cult members infected the salad bars of local restaurants, poisoning four-bean salads, pea salads, and even the most sacred of foods: macaroni.

Seven hundred and fifty-one people were poisoned in the attack, making it the biggest biological attack in American history. When it didn't work, they attempted to assassinate the US Attorney for the District of Oregon, who was looking into criminal activity of the movement. Which, given the assassination attempts, was fair.

After a number of convictions – including that of Rajneesh's trusty sidekick Sheela – Rajneesh was eventually deported in 1985. The cult declined in the following decades, likely due to recruiters having to pause their sales pitch about enlightenment to say, 'Now, you're going to hear an awful lot of things about shitting.'

SIR BASIL ZAHAROFF

Zaharoff was an arms dealer, a field in which to truly distinguish yourself, you have to be a real piece of shit. To be named the world's worst arms dealer is like being named as the worst of the *Mrs Brown's Boys* cast, a challenge which Sir Basil Zaharoff (of course he was made a sir) was more than up to.

In November 1927, Sir Basil Zaharoff – then seventy-eight years old and one of the richest people in the world – spent two full days at his Paris mansion burning every last one of his diaries. Little pro tip: if your father or grandpa decides to set aside a few days to burn the records of what took place in his life, you probably don't need to ask him 'So what did you do in your youth?' to know it was bad.

Born in Greece in 1849, Zaharoff began his career as he meant to go on, as part of the Constantinople (now Istanbul) Fire Brigade. That may sound like a nice thing to do with your career, but Zaharoff's job was to light fires on purpose so that the corrupt team could profit by putting them out again and rescuing the occupants' belongings.[1]

Not much is known about his comings and goings at this point (due to the fact that he burned all his records in a fire. But hey, credit for doing it on a not-for-profit basis). However, what we do know is he worked for a time as a confidence trickster in America, and married a Philadelphia heiress under the name 'Prince Zacharias Basileus Zacharoff', which came as a shock to his other wife who he had married in Britain some thirteen years earlier. He also worked on the railroads in America, building up a fortune under the name of 'Count Zacharoff'.

Already having conquered the worlds of big business, imaginary titles and bigamy, he turned his attention to arms dealing, where he really began to excel. Selling arms for Vickers of Britain, he realised more money could be made if he simply escalated various conflicts currently taking place. The biggest coup of his career came when he sold an incredibly dodgy steam-powered submarine to Greece in 1886, knowing that it would scare the shit out of Turkey, with whom they were constantly in a standoff.[2] No major powers were interested in the submarine, because it was extremely unstable underwater – the prime environment of a fucking submarine. It would also overheat to the point that the crew were prone to fainting, making it more of an underwater trauma centre than a weapon.

Repeat business was not Zaharoff's goal on this one, but he knew that if he sold the submarine to Greece, Turkey would feel threatened and would, in turn, also want to buy the submarine (they ended up buying two). From here he went to Russia, where he was able to convince them that Greece and Turkey were now a threat due to the submarines they had, thus convincing the Russians to buy two of the pieces of crap. None of them worked or saw action, other than one of the Turkish vessels, which test-fired a torpedo and capsized itself, sinking to the ocean floor.

After a stint of arming the shit out of whoever asked during the First World War, and being honoured for his troubles, Zaharoff went back to his old ways of stirring up conflicts so he could profit from the carnage. He claimed that he persuaded Greece to push into a weakened Turkey, which resulted in heavy losses for Greece, and a hasty retreat – something that's only good for 1) Turkey, and 2) whoever the hell is selling weapons to Greece, which had now just royally pissed off a neighbour.

'I made wars so that I could sell arms to both sides,' Zaharoff once said, in what he apparently thought was a good sentence. 'I must have sold more arms than anyone else in the world.'

THE MAN WHO PRETENDED HE HADN'T JUST LOST A LION IN BIRMINGHAM CITY CENTRE

One of the most relatable assholes I've come across is a tamer of lions who ran a circus in the UK in 1889, was incredibly shit at his job, and got into worse trouble while attempting to cover his tracks.

Frank C. Bostock was the son of a circus owner, and by the time he was fifteen he desperately wanted to escape the family profession. However, one day during his summer holidays from priest school, he saw his father's lion tamer being extremely cruel to one of the lions. The lion mauled the tamer, and this was apparently the moment Frank decided to have a crack at lion taming after all. Having later run his decision by his father, and subsequently been told the nineteenth-century equivalent of 'fuck off', Frank climbed into the lion cage anyway. His dad saw him in there one day, and naturally threatened to beat the shit out of him if he ever made it out alive. However, when Frank showed quite a knack for not dying in a lion's cage, his father downgraded his thrashing to merely letting the boy get into a cage with a lion night after night. A lion, you might remember, which had recently mauled a colleague to fucking pieces.

Frank took to the road with the circus for several years, loving the circus life until one small problem emerged: one of the menagerie's two lions was an absolute dick. To be fair, wouldn't you be if you were ripped from your home in Africa and, every night, placed in a cage with a piece of food that won't stay still.

'He killed one man, and wounded several attendants,' Frank wrote in his book.[1] Being kind to the lion didn't work. Punishing it didn't work. The only way to keep it from mauling people was to appease it at all times.

One day, while the circus was passing the city of Birmingham, Frank and his team failed at this very task. The lion, highly agitated, broke loose from his cage and headed right for the city centre, which held around two hundred thousand Brummies at the time.

Scaring the crap out of a few ye olde Brummies as it went, the lion headed for an opening in the sewers, where it began to prowl. It made its way through the city underground, occasionally stopping to roar at every manhole it came to.

Nobody was shitting it more than Frank, however, who was responsible for the lion, as well as anyone the lion killed. Now here's where Frank becomes a highly relatable asshole. Imagine you've fucked up at work but have a chance to cover your tracks. For example, say you've lost an original file, but you still have a decent copy that you *might* be able to pass off as the real deal. Would you do it? Well, Frank had a second lion.

Bostock instructed his crew to take the second lion – in a covered cage – to one of the openings of the sewers. He then made a show of searching around the sewers for the first lion, and *pretended that he had found it* and moved it back into the cage. Everybody believed that the lion had been caught, and began swanning around Birmingham once again, no longer worrying about being mauled by a fucking lion, and merely resuming their musings on how terrible it was to be from Birmingham.

You would think that Frank would have come to his senses at some point, given how, if the first lion began roaring again, nobody was going to think it was, coincidentally, another lion that just happened to want to see the Bull Ring, or whatever the hell Birmingham's second tourist attraction is. However, Frank stayed silent as the crowds began to carry him on their shoulders chanting, 'They've got it! They've got the lion!' like he was a hero.

The crowd piled into Frank's show to see the hero lion tamer, while he absolutely shat it. While newspapers as far away as New Zealand[2] wrote about what a hero he was, he spent the night practising his best 'I'm not thinking about a lion lurking in the sewers that's about to maul some kid' expression. It wasn't until the next day – when a police officer thanked him for his bravery – that Frank broke down and confessed to pretending that a lion that had tasted human blood wasn't on the loose, getting hungrier and hungrier as time went on.

There was redemption to be had for Frank, however. With the assistance of five hundred armed men and many dogs, organised by the police, he headed back into the sewers once more and actually attempted to rescue the lion (he clearly must have been lacking a third lion). Using fireworks, he managed to corner it. One of the boarhounds, which he had let fight the lion on his behalf, then became quite injured, and so Bostock decided to fight the lion himself. He took off his jackboots and placed them over his hands, and asked for a kettle – which had been used to bring down supplies – to be placed over his head. Fortunately for Frank, the kettle fell off his head – being, as it was, a massive fucking kettle. The clanging noise terrified the lion, sending it running to a place where it could be trapped and brought back to its cage.

This time when Frank emerged from the sewer, actually heroic, the reaction from the crowds was nowhere near approaching the cheers they gave him when he set a lion loose on them and then pretended everything was fine. Which just goes to show how you should always try to be a fucking weasel.

OLIVER CROMWELL

It's difficult to lead an uprising against a king, shortly before killing him, and then be remembered primarily for something else. But outside of England, Cromwell is best known not for making Charles I a little bit shorter and a whole lot more dead, but for his attempt to re-conquer Ireland.

Cromwell hated the Irish, mostly due to their loyalty to the Roman Catholic Church. Fresh from his victory over Royalist forces in England, he was chosen to take command of the English campaign in Ireland, and was motivated in part by revenge for the alleged crimes of Catholic forces against Protestants during the Irish Rebellion of 1641, and also by a want to end anti-Protestant discrimination. Cromwell, who believed that God had guided him to victory in England, now apparently thought that God wanted him to slaughter Catholics by their thousands, in clear evidence that God – should he exist – needs to pipe up a bit more when it's time for everyone to cool their tits.

The first and biggest challenge to Cromwell was at the County Louth town of Drogheda in 1649, where 2,550 Royalists and Irish Confederate troops gathered to defend Ireland's eastern ports,[1] led by Arthur Aston. Aston believed that anybody who could take Drogheda could take Hell, given how well fortified it was. At the very least, he thought he could delay Cromwell while Royalist troops regrouped elsewhere.

If there's anyone who could take Hell, however, it was someone as Satany as Cromwell. Bar a few aesthetic differences, e.g. the horns, Cromwell and Satan had a lot in common in terms of sheer bloodlust. Six thousand men were ordered to attack Drogheda. They first battered the walls of the town with siege artillery pieces on 10 September 1649, and by the following day the walls had been breached.

When inside, Cromwell's troops were merciless. Catholic priests and friars hid in the steeple of St Peter's Church, where they were promptly burned alive. Many of the troops inside had surrendered, hoping for some sort of mercy from a man who had just burned actual priests to death, but they were executed nonetheless. Around two thousand people were killed in the massacre.

Any mass killing would be incomplete without providing a creepy quote about how the massacred deserved it because they displeased God, and Cromwell gladly obliged. 'I am persuaded that this is a righteous judgement of God upon these barbarous wretches, who have imbrued their hands in so much innocent blood and that it will tend to prevent the effusion of blood for the future,' he wrote of the campaign, 'which are satisfactory grounds for such actions, which otherwise cannot but work remorse and regret.'[2]

God wasn't quite done with Cromwell yet, sending him to Wexford to slaughter the town during peaceful surrender negotiations in the following month. Cromwell and Colonel David Synnot – who led the defence at Wexford – were negotiating surrender terms, while Cromwell had the town under siege. Cromwell became tired of waiting, and on 10 October went back to his old wall-smashing ways, like a fucking homicidal Kool-Aid mascot. Synnot decided to lay down arms and allow for the troops to enter the town. However, he had some new terms which Cromwell found unacceptable: he wanted his own troops to be able to withdraw and move to New Ross (a nearby town), and guarantees that the Catholic clergy in Wexford be not brutally murdered to death. To this, Cromwell responded by bombarding the shit out of Wexford again.

When the wall was breached and negotiations broke down, the commander of the castle ordered the surrender. Cromwell's men showed up and attacked and slaughtered any troops that hadn't fled, before plundering the town and killing plenty of civilians, just like God would have wanted.

JEANNE DE CLISSON

Jeanne de Clisson was a wealthy noblewoman, born in France at around the turn of the fourteenth century. Unlike most nobles, Clisson would go on to become a bloodthirsty pirate, slaughtering aristocrats on a rampage of revenge, rather than sit around in luxury and say a lot of French things about cake.

After two marriages didn't work out, one because the Pope annulled it and another largely because 50 per cent of the participants became dead, Jeanne met and married Olivier IV de Clisson, a warrior and wealthy Breton living in Nantes. Together, they had five children. She was very attached to him, much more so than his head was about to be to his body.

Following several battles with England in which the French lost, King Philip VI looked for people to blame. It's not clear whether Olivier had defected to the English[1] – some sources suggest he had been captured and then released at a low ransom, raising suspicions – or whether the Duke of Brittany, Charles de Blois, incorrectly believed him to have defected. Either way, the effect was the same: his head needed to come off.

In a trial scant of evidence, Olivier was condemned to death, before his body was desecrated and displayed in public. Jeanne de Clisson was not keen. She took her children to see her husband's head, displayed as it was on a pike. Supposedly, this was to sear hatred into their hearts, though as someone with kids I'd say it was possible she'd merely run out of ideas for a day out.

Next, she sold all her husband's lands and properties, in order to raise enough money for an army, with hopefully a few quid set aside for the inevitable therapy your children will need when you take them to 'Dad's head on pike' instead of Disneyland. She swore vengeance on King Philip and Charles de Blois, and began her attack. She gathered four hundred men[2] and attacked a castle held by a supporter of de Blois. She and her army slaughtered everyone inside the castle, bar one. According to legend – I say legend because, let's face it, it all seems a little too *Kill Bill* to be the actual truth – this began her signature move of leaving one victim alive to tell everyone else what they saw.

Following some risky land-based attacks that could have ended in disaster, Jeanne got piratey. She purchased warships, including her flagship *Ma Revanche*, or 'My Revenge', and started a ten-year campaign of destroying French ships in the English Channel, which may have contributed somewhat to confirming de Blois' suspicions about her husband's loyalties. In the first two years of the campaign, she kept several of her children aboard the warship, then her boat was sunk and one of her sons died before rescue could arrive. Learning her lesson (taking kids to war = bad), she set sail once more, this time without her children, murdering the shit out of any French vessels she passed, be they warships or merchant vessels.

After her run of vengeance was over, and with the support of England, she was able to retire and marry once more, before dying in 1359, aged fifty-nine. Which isn't a bad lifespan for a treasonous pirate who was wanted by a king.

Jeanne's tale of vengeance wasn't quite over, however, as one of her less forgetful sons hadn't quite recovered from seeing his dad's head with a spike where the neck would usually be. Olivier V, who would become known as 'The Butcher' which is the mark of a psychopath for anyone whose job isn't actually selling sausages, managed to end up in an attack on Charles de Blois himself. The attack saw de Blois separated from the French army, whereupon he was brutally murdered.

Lessons we can take from this tale? Some assholes are kind of cool.

EMPEROR ZHENGDE

Inheriting thrones is a terrible idea for so many reasons. It's undemocratic, for instance. Or, instead of fair government, your prince son (and, one day, successor) might only be interested in shagging.

In 1505, following the death of his father, Zhu Houzhao became emperor of the whole of China aged just fourteen, too young to even watch *RoboCop* or *Freddy Got Fingered*. It soon became clear that, like most teenage boys, he wasn't really interested in ruling the whole of China. His interests lay elsewhere, if you know what I mean. If you don't know what I mean, imagine me winking and pointing directly at a fanny.

Taking the name 'Zhengde', meaning 'right virtue', the horndog began doing everything he could to avoid any actual governing, including copious amounts of doing sex, and getting the shit mauled out of him by tigers. He would go on tiger-hunting trips for weeks at a time, once getting mauled to the point where he couldn't attend court for a month.[1]

While peasants probably wondered, 'What the hell?' Zhengde created '*Bao Fang*' palaces, which translates as 'The Leopards' Chamber' in which he would house leopards and tigers. When he grew bored of this, or, perhaps, became a little grumpy from the maulings, he replaced the large cats with the far more safe option of a shitload of women. From the women's perspective, of course, this was not safer, as his harem became so large that many of them starved to death due to a lack of food.[2] Essentially, there were so many women he wanted to have sex with, that nobody in his court could come up with a robust enough rationing system to cope.

While his women died of starvation, Zhengde would often just abandon court altogether – like how kids forget about certain toys – and spend his time outside the city, while ministers would desperately attempt to persuade him to come home. This was probably preferable to him being around, however, seeing as he was a massive asshole and all.

In another one of his batshit escapades, he once set up a fake commercial district and forced his ministers to act like merchants while he pretended to be a commoner, sort of like a reverse Aladdin. Anyone who didn't comply would be punished. During battle he was even less mature, forcing captured prisoners to wear the various body parts of their fallen friends, before displaying their dismembered genitals in public for reasons best not asked of a man who likes to put dicks on display.

In what was probably quite a good move, considering his main interests were being kooky and having it off with prostitutes, Zhengde chose to leave most decisions in the hands of his eunuchs, though several became corrupt and rinsed him for all the money they could, before he eventually caught wind and executed them.

Needless to say, China didn't fare too well during Zhengde's reign, particularly in the south, which wasn't adequately represented by his eunuchs. He continued to bang his way through his rule for a full sixteen years before dying of an illness he caught through getting off his tits before taking a fall off a boat, learning precisely fuck-all from a previous fall off a boat.

THE REPUBLICAN WHO ESSENTIALLY MADE HIMSELF KING

As much as it might seem like the right thing to do to get rid of monarchical rule before all the incest produces a Joffrey (or, for fans of real life, a Hapsburg), revolutionaries have asked the question 'Well, what shall we replace it with?' and, historically, have tended to respond with 'Some kind of gigantic Cromwell', which happens to be a synonym for 'cunt'. (For more on Cromwell see page 85.) The brief period following the execution of Louis XVI in 1793 France – thanks to Maximilien Robespierre – was no exception.

In the beginning, Robespierre was not such a bad *mec* (which Google Translate tells me is French for dude). He campaigned for 'universal manhood suffrage', which meant men from all corners of society were allowed to vote, and involved a lot less penis pain than the name implies. He also campaigned for the end of slavery, putting some pretty firm marks in the 'not a shit' tally. He even acted as a public prosecutor and advocate for commoners to be integrated into public life, in order to agitate and strengthen the revolution against Louis XVI and his cake wife, Marie Antoinette, calling for them to be overthrown for treason as head of the revolutionary group, the Jacobins.[1] But after the French Revolution, known in France at the time as just the regular revolution (in the same way that you don't say 'I'm going through an Italian break-up' or 'How goes the English piles?'), Robespierre gained a reputation for taking the whole revolution thing a bit too far.

A few years prior, on 27 July 1793, he was elected head of the 'Committee of Public Safety', which, despite what the name might suggest, was the cause of many a guillotining. The modern-day equivalent, if I had to suggest one, would be a lifeguard harpooning a paddler in the splash pool. Unfortunately for the leaders of the revolution, it turns out that executing the king wasn't like killing the head vampire (Dracula) and turning all the shitter vampires (Captain Sparkles from *Twilight*) to dust. There were a lot of problems, and a lot of counterrevolutionaries trying to undo the revolutionaries' hard work – not exactly popping Louis' head back on, but at least replicating some of the horrendous power structures the king had put in place.

Robespierre and the committee channelled their inner king, and began to rule the country as a virtual dictatorship, a period that would come to be known as *la Terreur* (the Reign of Terror). They declared France to be 'revolutionary until peace',[2] giving themselves powers to use violence against their own citizens until threats to the revolution were over.

Once you've passed your initial 'It's fine for me to death the shit out of you if you protest' legislation, it's amazing how any further protest becomes ineffective. The committee, led by Robespierre, passed more laws calling counterrevolutionaries and anybody who aided them (for example, through spreading falsehoods or sheltering monarchists) 'enemies of the people'.[3] The punishment for anyone found guilty of the new crime was death, with no distinctions between people picking up arms and yelling '*j'adore* kings' before embarking on a pro-king rampage, and those who had written a letter to the committee expressing worries about the revolutionaries getting 'quite murdery'. Before all of this kicked off, Robespierre had earned a reputation as a lawyer who defended the poor. Now his committee had made it law that anybody accused of being an 'enemy of the people' was not allowed a lawyer to defend them during their tribunal.

'If virtue be the spring of a popular government in times of peace, the spring of that government during a revolution is virtue combined with terror: virtue, without which terror is destructive; terror, without which virtue is impotent,' Robespierre said,[4] in a speech that wouldn't look out of place being delivered by the villain in a Jean-Claude Van Damme movie titled *Cop Justice*. 'Terror is only justice: prompt, severe and inflexible; it is then an emanation of virtue; it is less a distinct principle than a natural consequence of the general principle of democracy, applied to the most pressing wants of the country.'

It turned out that executing and imprisoning people like you're paid per unit of human suffering set something of a bad precedent.[5] It turned out to be a bad idea on a purely personal level too. Following his assistance in the arrest of fellow revolutionary friends, Robespierre made a speech about internal enemies, scaring the shit out of fellow revolutionaries who remembered the arrest and execution of the fellow revolutionary friends mentioned at the start of this sentence. His fellow revolutionaries turned on Robespierre, rather than waiting patiently to be accused and executed by him. Robespierre soon found himself on the wrong end of a guillotine in 1794, along with over a hundred of his supporters. Still, at least it showed he was willing to get his hands dirty for the sake of the revolution, by being publicly executed for the cause.

CARAVAGGIO

If you're a good enough painter, people will forget that time you killed someone while attempting to cut their dick off. I should immediately point out that I know of only one time this has been the case, and it was with one of the greatest painters of all time. So if you are planning on taking someone's penis off, don't blame me if your watercolours don't cut the mustard.

Caravaggio, swanning around Italy in the early seventeenth century, was lucky to be talented in one of those professions where being really good at something apparently gives you licence to be an absolute asshole – painting. Or at least, so thought Caravaggio. I'm not kidding. A contemporary of Caravaggio described his usual work pattern as 'After a fortnight's work he will swagger about for a month or two with a sword at his side and a servant following him, from one ball-court to the next, ever ready to engage in a fight or an argument, so that it is most awkward to get along with him.'[1] Basically, imagine if you'd filled in a really good spreadsheet at work, then spent the next few weeks wandering about, looking for someone to twat.

He had a terrible temper, as well as being a bit of a jerk.[2] From time to time, he would roam the streets with a sword on display, or swear at police officers out of boredom. Though that may make him sound cool, one time he also threw a plate into the face of a waiter because his artichokes were undercooked. I realise that was in a time before the phrase 'Don't shoot the messenger', but when you're mad at the chef, basic restaurant etiquette dictates that you don't crockery the waiter.

Caravaggio was also sued by fellow painter Giovanni Baglione after he wrote a plethora of offensive poems about him, and they didn't even fucking rhyme.

Where he really surpassed himself, however, was when he accidentally murdered someone in 1606, possibly while attempting to cut off his aforementioned penis. For years, it was thought that Caravaggio lost his shit during a *pallacorda* match (think tennis, but with ye olde racquets), and killed Ranuccio Tommasoni while attempting to cut his penis off during an ensuing duel. While things like this would certainly make Wimbledon watchable, some historians believe that the fight was actually over a woman: a prostitute who posed for many of Caravaggio's paintings. Tommasoni was her pimp. 'Particular wounds in Roman street fights meant particular things,' art historian Andrew Graham-Dixon told the *Telegraph*. 'If a man insulted another man's reputation he might have his face cut. If a man insulted a man's woman he would get his penis cut off.'

It's probable that Caravaggio wasn't trying to kill Tommasoni, but was attempting to cut off his penis and slipped, catching his femoral artery. Not that the 'I was trying to chop his dick off, officer' defence was likely to work very well on the constables he repeatedly called cunts.

Caravaggio was forced to flee (slightly) from Rome to Naples, or face execution for his crime, as decreed by the Pope. However, as he had thus far been able to do any old shit and get away with it because he was good at sloshing around paint, Caravaggio believed he was so talented that he could paint his way out of this mess, sending free paintings to the Pope as penance for his crimes. Sorry about the whole murder thing, I done drawn you a cat.

CHARLES X

In 1625, French and English pirates began to use the French colony in Tortuga (northern Haiti) as a nice place to make camp. Entertaining pirates with all the violence and fucking shanties that this involved would become known as 'the good old days' to the people of Tortuga, compared to what was to come.

When the French first came to set up colonies in the country in 1665, following occupation by the Spanish, they found that they didn't have enough workers on the island to exploit the natural resources. This was largely due to the extermination of the native population that had happened thanks to Columbus' previous efforts, followed by those of Portugal. (For more on Columbus, see pages 20–1.) As such, France shipped in a second group of exploited people: slaves, mainly from West Africa, given that France was heavily involved in the transport of slaves to the Caribbean anyway.[1] The conditions in Haiti for growing valuable goods – such as sugar, coffee and cotton – in combination with France's not giving a shit about forcing humans to work for free, made Haiti into France's richest colony. This continued for quite some time, before it all fell apart when the slaves began to revolt in 1804.

The conditions for the slaves were awful, even in comparison to the treatment of slaves elsewhere around the world, which is like being told 'Fuck me, calm down' by Fred West. One former slave, explaining why they revolted in 1804 against the French population, alluded to the cruel conditions. 'Have they not hung up men with heads downward, drowned them in sacks, crucified them on planks, buried them alive, crushed them in mortars? Have they not forced them to eat excrement?' he wrote.[2] 'Have they not thrown them into boiling cauldrons of cane syrup? Have they not put men and women inside barrels studded with spikes and rolled them down mountainsides into the abyss?' The average lifespan for slaves in the country was twenty-one years.

The people of Haiti began to rebel against French rule, but France did not back down easily. Contrary to the nation's image of surrendering at the merest hint of fisticuffs, France fought hard to retain its cash cow, before eventually Napoleon Bonaparte's forces were distracted by a second war with Britain (if there's one thing France and Britain love, it's warring the shit out of each other), and were defeated by Haiti.

Unfortunately, Haiti was not left in a great position after declaring independence in 1804, most of its resources having been destroyed during the fighting of the previous twelve years. Now came the real dick move from France: King Charles X (who came to the throne in 1824) called for reparations to be paid for the loss of his colony and slaves. He demanded a hundred million francs,[3] or around £17 billion in today's money. Rather than being able to focus on creating a prosperous independent nation, the former slaves would spend the next century trying to pay back slavers for the crime of not wanting to be slaves. It's the equivalent of a school bully charging you 'not beating the shit out of you' money in return for the cessation of beatings.

The debt kept accruing interest, which meant that Haiti was spending around 80 per cent of its budget on loan repayments by 1900, nearly a century after independence.[4] It would take until 1947 to pay off the debt to a dead king. Even zombies don't want to harm you fiscally.

THE WORLD'S BIGGEST MISER

Hetty Green was a trailblazer of sorts, proving in highly misogynistic nineteenth-century America that women could be ruthless money-grabbing assholes just as effectively as any man, if not much more so. By the time of her death, she was the richest woman in the world, worth over $2 billion in today's money. You'd think with that kind of money, you'd pay for things like heating or basic preventative medicine to stop your son's leg being amputated, but you'd be wrong on two counts.

Green was born into a wealthy family, who had made their money by killing the fuck out of whales with their whaling fleet. She soon entered the family business, taking over the accounts for the firm by the age of thirteen,[1] an age where most are more concerned with school and cooties than tax returns for whale blubber. Though she didn't directly take part in the spearing of whales, I imagine she at least allowed herself a *kerching* noise every time one got stabbed.

With her family's wealth behind her, Green started to make a fortune of her own as she grew. She had a talent for numbers, a shitload of money, and – the most important ingredient – a second shitload of money. Her ethos was quite simple: she'd buy up a lot of property or stock – she particularly liked railroad stocks and mortgage bonds – when nobody wanted it, then waited until it was popular again and would sell it for massively inflated prices. She had plenty of money to keep her afloat in the meantime, so the wait didn't really affect her. It was, to a large extent, a classic case of having money makes you money.

She was a smart investor too, buying up stocks that she believed had been undervalued by the market, and selling them later when she knew them to be overvalued. She also specialised in loaning banks – and even cities – large amounts of money (with interest, of course) during crashes, foreclosing on companies that couldn't repay loans, and was often seen as a fancy loan shark.

Green was stingy throughout her life, refusing to pay for heating and other necessities. She also refused to pay for treatment of a hernia because it would cost about 0.00000000000000000001 per cent of her worth. Instead she chose the method of calling the doctors all 'a bunch of robbers' and jamming a stick against her hernia.[2] But where her stinginess really shone through was when her son's leg was injured as a child. He had been hit by another child, who was riding a cart pulled by a dog, a detail so weird that I'm legally obliged to include it. The richest woman in the world, rather than get her son to a hospital immediately, took her time and looked around for the nearest free clinic that would provide free treatment to those in poverty. The staff working there recognised her, and demanded payment, at which point Hetty remarked (I imagine), 'Well, fuck my son's leg then,' and left. Not long afterwards, his leg needed to be amputated because of gangrene. His father, a man with very little money left, paid for it, rather than attempt to get his ex to cough up.

When Green died, aged eighty-one, in 1916, her son claimed that she wasn't as stingy as all that, which must have been quite hard to believe coming from someone who was standing there on the only leg remaining to him, on account of his mother's stinginess. He claimed that she had donated to many charities, though none came forward to verify this and he couldn't name a single one. He also said that she had kept on an employee who was not fit for work, out of the kindness of her heart, though his fellow employees remember her quite quickly telling the man to fuck off after realising he could no longer work (OK, she merely fired him, but, to be fair, I'd argue that's a much more ruthless business equivalent of telling somebody to fuck off).

Before she died, she earned herself the moniker the 'Witch of Wall Street', which is obviously misogynistic. But she was nevertheless an asshole.

THE CIA AGENTS TURNED PRANKSTERS

The CIA is well known for its absolutely batshit schemes – from attempting to assassinate Castro with an exploding cigar to trying to kill goats using only their minds. They are usually a jarring mix of something you'd find scrawled in the dream diary of a convicted serial killer (in excrement, of course, the serial killer's ink) and an episode of *Scooby-Doo*.

Of particular 'I would have gotten away with it if it wasn't for you meddling guerrillas' vibes was a scheme hatched in the Philippines in 1950, led by Air Force Brigadier General Edward G. Lansdale. The CIA took a break from its usual schtick of propping up pro-American administrations in a bid to suppress communism in order to do the exact same thing but, this time, by tricking the locals into thinking they were being attacked by vampires.

At the time, much of the Philippines was rural and the inhabitants were quite superstitious. One superstition the CIA felt they could use to their advantage was that of the Aswang. If you're unfamiliar with the Aswang, they're shapeshifting demons that can take on any form, from dogs to witches, and beautiful women who happen to be bloodsucking vampires, concealing a massive proboscis-like tongue with which to slurp up your blood.[1]

It was the vampire form of the Aswang that the CIA decided to use to trick the locals. All they needed was a victim, and the ghoul-like willingness to drain them entirely of their blood. First, they spread a rumour amongst the residents of the provinces of Pampanga, Nueva Ecija and Tarlac, where resident Huks – a group of communist guerrillas – were causing trouble for them. The rumour was that Aswang were roaming in the hills. Then came Part Two. 'When a Huk patrol made up of several men came along the trail, the ambushers silently snatched the last man of the patrol, their move unseen in the dark night,' Lansdale wrote of his and the CIA's activities.[2] 'They punctured his neck with two holes, vampire-fashion, held the body up by the heels, drained it of blood, and put the corpse back on the trail.'

I'd like you to take a moment to note that Lansdale wrote this in a memoir, a format generally reserved for anecdotes about meeting minor celebrities, before we move on. Imagine Laurence Llewelyn-Bowen slipping in a detailed description of how he and Handy Andy donned werewolf costumes and ritually slew a contestant on *Changing Rooms*.

'When the Huks returned to look for the missing man and found their bloodless comrade, every member of the patrol believed that an Aswang had got him and that one of them would be next if they remained on that hill. When daylight came, the whole Huk squadron moved out of the vicinity.'[3]

Over four years,[4] the CIA spent its time puncturing the necks of people and animals, leaving the carcasses to scare the shit out of the locals, and occasionally left all-seeing 'eye of god' paintings opposite the houses of those they believed to be Huk sympathisers.

The Huk eventually lost their grip on the area, due to a myriad of factors, but nevertheless the CIA chalked up their Aswang tactic as a success. Though I'd argue that it's equally likely they thought, 'Fucking hell, the mad bastards are draining the blood of the slain now, might be time to skedaddle.'

THE STRAW HAT RIOTERS

As if life wasn't difficult enough back in the nineteenth and early twentieth centuries, society developed a shitload of rules about what you should put on your head while you waited to die of dysentery or war.

In America, it became a tradition (thanks to fashion) that you should only wear straw hats during the summer boating season (hence the term 'boater'). This wasn't some rule that would merely get you a bit of a look if you broke it. If you were spotted wearing a hat past 15 September, strangers would ridicule you, as well as take the hat off your head and stomp on it. In today's terms, it would be like if you wore a Christmas jumper on 2 January and a mob tore it off your body and shat on it, to let you know that *you* had made a faux pas.

For a bizarre amount of time, everyone just accepted that this was fine. If you wore your hat too long, strangers would smash it to fucking pieces and then you'd get sunburn – and that would be your fault.

Then, in 1922, a gang of teenagers decided that they couldn't wait a further two days to stamp on hats, and on 13 September went on a 'straw hat smashing orgy'[1] that lasted through the night, involving hundreds of youths.[2] The police were called; many were arrested and seven were spanked by their parents at the police station. Apparently, while ripping the hat off someone on the 15th was merely met with a nod of approval, two days earlier than that and it could land you in the fucking slammer.

To be fair, the teenagers did more than enough to earn their place in prison. The gangs, which eventually numbered into the hundreds according to reports at the time, were armed with sticks with nails at the end. They would threaten straw hat fans and tell them to run, forcing them to bump into another gang who would try to snatch the hats off their heads for fun. Imagine someone coming at you with a mace for the crime of wearing a fedora (real though that crime is).

Though the riots were largely non-violent, they continued over several days and there were a number of beatings and attacks on those who attempted to defend their hat for the extra two days before it could legitimately be twatted off their head on the 15th. The police, to add to the absurdity, went out in plain clothes and straw hats in order to entrap rioters. This resulted in one policeman having his hat knocked off by a rioter, running down the road and tripping into a gutter, which was enough to charge the hat thief for assault.

The rioter explained to the magistrate that he didn't know that his victim was a policeman before he pulled out his revolver in order to threaten him for wearing a hat. Very much the 'As I explained before, I was trying to attack the vulnerable' defence.

Several people were hospitalised by the fairly severe beatings. Despite this, the tradition of knocking people's hats off and stomping on them continued for some years, until the hats fell out of fashion for being shite.

THE FRUIT COMPANY THAT PUT BANANAS BEFORE WORKERS' RIGHTS

Colonial powers, you'll be shocked to hear, had a wealth of tools available to them to suppress the countries they were colonising – the biggest of these tools being wealth. A classic move was to march into a country where people are largely self-sufficient and announce 'You only make sugar now' or some other valuable crop. Over time, staples (for example, millet and quinoa in Rwanda) that locals relied on for, you know, food, were replaced with more valuable non-indigenous crops.[1] For the colonisers, this had the advantage of 'them getting the stuff they like', and then cramming it into their mouths. On the downside, the colonised now had crops that were more susceptible to failure, and when that happened famine was likely. What's more, the countries often specialised as agricultural economies, relying on the export of crops, which didn't increase in value in the same way exports in fully industrialised nations did. It's what was known as a good old-fashioned coloniser triple fuck.

One notable example of this getting way out of hand is the several wars fought over bananas in the nineteenth century. In this case, the bulk of the evil was carried out by United Fruit, which is a pretty innocuous name for something that would result in so much human suffering, like if Hannibal Lecter was named Mr Nibbles instead.

Minor Cooper Keith, born 19 January 1848, started his banana business small, planting a few cuttings in Costa Rica in the 1870s.[2] He soon realised he could make insane amounts of profit out of the (in my opinion) barely edible fruit, if he could grow them in enough quantities, and create railroads to slam the fruit into hungry American mouths. More importantly, he needed a government that was happy to exploit the absolute shit out of workers to farm the bananas, and who would turn a blind eye to poor working conditions for that sweet banana buck. This is where United Fruit came in.

'Guatemala was chosen as the site for the company's earliest development activities,' a former United Fruit executive said of their first major step into the business of selling bananas and committing massive human rights abuses,[3] 'because at the time we entered Central America, Guatemala's government was the region's weakest, most corrupt and most pliable.' The company set up shop across central America and the Caribbean, creating exploitative banana-based export economies. The amount of money they brought into the countries (and straight into the hands of the ruling class) afforded them a lot of leeway when it came to paying taxes and exploitation of the work force.

Unsurprisingly, workers in the Dominican Republic, Haiti, Guatemala, or basically any country whose flag you've seen on a banana sticker, rebelled against the company and went on strike. The workers soon found that they not only had to contend with their own pro-Big Banana governments (or banana republics, as they became known) but America too. The American army crushed strikes in Honduras and Haiti throughout the twentieth century, or fought revolution from 'Can you stop making us produce bananas for a pittance?' types, of course with the backing of local governments who were heavily invested in not being at the Louis XVI end of a revolution.

Guatemala, where the government could usually be counted upon to e.g. force the unemployed to do labour for a hundred days a year, or allow landowners to take any action including executing their workers, received help from the US to keep its presidents alive and working in the interests of United Fruit.

When the democratic and left-leaning president Árbenz began to try to improve workers' rights in the 1950s, United Fruit began heavily lobbying for the current Guatemalan government to be overthrown on the grounds that they were massive communists.

Whether the Eisenhower government believed them, or whether it merely wanted to protect business interests, the US intervened and helped to overthrow a democratic government at the behest of a fruit company.[4] Say what you will about the Sun-Maid Girl – at least she's never ordered a military coup because she wasn't making enough money from raisins. To my knowledge.

ACTION PARK

The next asshole is an amusement park, which I realise makes me sound a tad unhinged. I can't imagine anybody would want to, e.g., make eye contact with someone standing outside the gates calling Thorpe Park a wanker. However, Action Park in Vernon Township, New Jersey, is thoroughly deserving of the title. Opening in 1978, the waterpark differed from other parks in three main areas: their willingness to let teenagers operate the rides, the fatality count and their tolerance of snakes in the water.[1]

Super speedboats

Pretty much rule one of driving a boat, if you don't listen to the shithead on the *Titanic*, is 'Don't treat the boat like a fucking bumper car'. However, that's what often happened when visitors flocked to the super speedboats ride which was located on a swamp in the park. To add an extra thrill for people who find the idea of being smashed to pieces by a boat travelling at 50mph 'a little humdrum', the swamp was filled with snakes. It's likely that the park staff were merely unable to keep pests under control, but who knows – don't you just wonder if maybe an employee at a staff meeting wrote 'Spice up the speedboats by adding cobras' on a whiteboard, before being met with rapturous applause.

In one crash between park staff after hours, a lifeguard had to jump in to rescue one of the drivers while the snakes chased him.

Battle action tanks

The last thing an amusement park needs is tanks, but that's what Action Park had. Guests could ride in the tanks and shoot tennis balls at each other, and disable other tanks if they hit their target. The problem was that when the tanks broke down – which was often – the employees would have to run out there to fix them, and it sort of became a tradition to shoot the crap out of them while they went, on purpose. It was like being an underpaid ball boy/girl for a malevolent Rafael Nadal.

The Cannonball Loop

Action Park took the unusual step of actually taking safety precautions on the Cannonball Loop, which should give you an idea of how likely you were to really hospitalise yourself if you were dumb enough to give it a go. The ride was essentially a big straight waterslide that ended in a tight loop the loop.

The testing phase, according to one of the former employees of the park, was to pay employees $100 to give it a crack. One man who took that offer told the outlet *Weird New Jersey*, '$100 did not buy enough booze to drown out that memory'. The ride was closed multiple times during the park's run, which isn't surprising given that several mannequins that were also used to test the ride ended up without limbs. Though nothing this dramatic happened to riders, there were quite a lot of injuries, and they ended up building an escape hatch to dig out people who got stuck in the loop.

The tidal wave pool

It was only a matter of time before the park saw several drownings. Speeding up the process was the tidal wave pool. The waves in this pool were so strong that, rather than simply turn down the dial, the park employed twelve lifeguards to watch the swimmers at all times. During busy times, up to thirty people were rescued per day – much more than the usual one or two per season at parks without water rides based on fucking tsunamis.

Unsurprisingly, the park eventually closed in 1996 due to the problems laid out above. It reopened again in 1998 under a different company name after a massive overhaul in safety regulations. One of the advert jingles for Action Park back in the day was, hilariously, 'There's nothing in the world like Action Park'. And hopefully there never will be again.

LEOPOLD II OF BELGIUM

As I mentioned in the introduction of this book, I've omitted a few of the really famous assholes for being too famous. Hitler and Stalin don't get their entries, for instance, as this would be like a DJ introducing 'hip new obscure band The Beatles'. However, Leopold II of Belgium will get his own chapter due to the fact that he was so much of an asshole that even other bloodthirsty colonialists took time out of their atrocities to condemn him in particular.

The Scramble for Africa is a strangely pleasant name for when seven European powers invaded Africa and then divided it up between themselves to rule. Kind of like if you called the act that started the Second World War the Clamber for Poland Before the Big Earth Ruckus. Leopold II of Belgium promised a humanitarian mission in Africa, and to improve African lives. European leaders gave him 770,000 square miles to create his own colony in 1885, which he would call the Congo Free State, now the Democratic Republic of Congo. However, Leopold missed out in his initial pitch that the improvement of lives would involve quite a bit of forced child labour, not to mention the removal of limbs for not hitting quarterly quotas. Not that it's the main thing here, but he clearly needed to work on his presentation skills if he left out these fairly major bullet points, although, in his defence, search results for accompanying clipart images of 'widespread mutilation' are somewhat lacking.

Leopold ran the colony as a fund for the person who really needed the money: future kings of Belgium who happened to be him. At first, exports of ivory failed to make much money for the colony, but then the rubber boom offered a canny opportunity for any moral vacuum of a person willing to force Congolese men to collect it before then taking the profits for themselves. Leopold introduced a system whereby labour could be taken as taxation, and sent his own army of mercenaries to get in on the action. Private companies in the country were allowed to collect this labour and maximise profits with very little state interference, which – shocker – generally doesn't end in a workers' utopia where everybody shares in the profits. Workers were treated incredibly badly, and were physically abused with whips on a regular basis, which probably seemed like Christmas compared to the other methods used for squeezing more rubber out of the slaves. For example, when workers failed to meet their rubber quotas, soldiers would regularly mutilate their children – removing their hands and feet. Soldiers would return with baskets of hands,[1] ensuring the slaves wouldn't rebel against them, and forever ruining a traditional picnic container.

They were rewarded for the collection of hands – from adults and children – as proof that they had killed those who had rebelled against Leopold, or provided insufficient rubber, which encouraged more mutilations by men so depraved they were willing to work for Leopold in the first place.

Children, on top of being seen merely as limbs with which to threaten their parents, did not fare well under Leopold's rule. Hostages were often taken for coercion purposes, while others were forced into child colonies where they would often die of diseases before they could be trained to be soldiers. Eventually, in 1908, European leaders – who were also exploiting the shit out of Africa – believed that Leopold's reign was too cruel to tolerate, even in comparison to their own cruel regimes. This must have been like receiving a lecture on animal cruelty by a man attempting to force a cat through a shredder, but nevertheless Leopold's reign was ended by Belgium, which punished him by taking away his colony through purchasing it with a lot of cash.

People who have since defended Leopold from accusations of atrocities on the grounds that he never went to Congo, which is a bit like defending a mass murderer because they took the trouble to hire an absolute bloodthirsty cunt of a hitman.

THOMAS MIDGLEY JR

Without knowing his motivations and purely looking at his life, you would think that Thomas Midgley Jr was a particularly depressed robot sent back in time to destroy humanity before we could invent the robot. Midgley was an engineer who developed his first planet-killer while working at General Motors in Detroit in 1921. At the time, 'knocking' was a common problem in cars, whereby a pocket of air/fuel mixture does not ignite in the proper place, causing a knocking sound as well as other engine problems. Midgley's bright idea of a solution was akin to a doctor setting fire to your face to cure acne.

The engineer added tetraethyl lead to gasoline, which, to be fair, stopped the knocking and improved engine performance.[1] Two years later, it was released under the brand name 'Ethyl', and no adverts mentioned what it contained for the same reason you wouldn't call a new tasty fruit drink 'cyanide juice': everybody knew it was incredibly poisonous.

We knew about lead poisoning around 2000 BC, in fact. Jesus himself could have said, 'Jesus Christ, we knew about that a whole Jesus ago.' For centuries, people had experienced horrendous symptoms caused by lead, from constipation and learning disabilities to comas, seizures and good old-fashioned death. As well as being known about in some manner for almost four thousand years, new symptoms were constantly being discovered. At the start of the twentieth century, it was discovered that women who worked in lead factories tended to be infertile, and any children they did give birth to did not survive long. Charles Dickens, while touring lead mills in London, wrote of one woman that 'her brain is coming out her ear and it hurts her dreadful'.[2]

Even if Midgley was somehow ignorant of all this, he very soon wouldn't be. Workers at the plants where Ethyl was produced started experiencing tremors, hallucinations and death in significant numbers. Five at the plant died – one while restrained in a straitjacket[3] – and they wouldn't be the last.

In order to prove that leaded petrol wasn't poisonous (which it was) Midgley conducted a demonstration in which he poured it all over his hands, then inhaled the gas for a minute. During his subsequent time off to recover from lead poisoning, he wrote to his boss to reiterate what a shitload of money they were going to make with this new invention, supposedly saying, 'Can you imagine how much money we're going to make with this? We're going to make two hundred million dollars, maybe even more.'[4]

With workers continuing to go insane, several cities in the US banned leaded petrol, or as they mistakenly called it, 'gas'. However, Midgley's colleagues appealed to the federal government to look into the impacts of lead with the help of industry scientists such as, oh I don't know, Thomas Midgley. People who had concerns about lead were excluded from the group, and they came down firmly in favour of not worrying about all the poisonings and deaths. In the end, the federal government overruled the cities that had banned lead, allowing for lead to be pumped into everyone's breathing holes once more.

His lust for killing still unsatisfied, Midgley's next planet-murderer came in the form of a fridge. Before Midgely, refrigerators tended to use refrigerants such as propane or sulphur dioxide. Honestly, this wasn't great due to how most people like a fridge that isn't going to fucking explode, which on top of destroying your house could really ruin your mayonnaise, so at least Midgley was trying to solve a real problem this time. However, his solution was to use dichlorodifluoromethane, or Freon 12 – the world's first chlorofluorocarbon, aka CFC, aka that thing that really helped rip our ozone layer to shreds.

As was his style at the time, Midgley breathed in this new gas to prove, once again, that it was safe. While it had no harmful effect on him, it's the environment that Freon was a problem for, so this is sort of like saying, 'See, this goldfish isn't drowning so it's safe for you to breathe underwater.'

In a twist surprising to nobody who had watched him huff bag after bag of his own dangerous inventions, Midgely was killed by one of his own creations. Towards the end of his life, he contracted polio, limiting his movement and very much taking him out of the 'Watch me huff this' game. Side note, but in many ways early chemical engineering was a precursor to *Jackass*. In order to help him get in and out of bed he created a system of ropes and pulleys, eventually becoming entangled and strangling himself, making it, out of all his inventions, the one with the lowest death count by some margin.

THE WOMAN WHO KEPT HER LOVERS IN THE ATTIC

Walburga 'Dolly' Korschel was born in 1880 in Germany, before moving to America early in her life to live the American dream: a nice home, a successful spouse, and some guy kept in the attic like a Christmas tree, should you ever require a bang.

In 1897, Dolly married Fred Oesterreich, who owned an apron factory in a time when everybody loved an apron, and both of them settled down in Milwaukee.[1] All was not bliss, however. Despite all the money and aprons you could possibly dream of, it turned out that owning an unlimited number of aprons couldn't make you come. Dolly was unsatisfied by her husband and had a string of affairs outside the house before she ordered in.

One day in 1913, she asked for her husband to send around one of his engineers – Otto Danhuber – in order to fix her sewing machine, in what was clearly a pre-war version of the pizza guy delivering pizza in pornography. When Otto showed up, she was wearing pretty much nothing, making it clear to him that the repair job was located entirely within her pants.

Despite the sixteen-year age gap – he was seventeen, she was thirty-three – the two kept up the affair for as long as they could,[2] first going to hotel rooms and then doing it in the house. Soon the neighbours grew suspicious of the typewriter guy going around every few days (What is this woman doing to her typewriters? How strong is her brand loyalty that she hasn't chucked out the twat?), so she told them that he was her 'vagabond half-brother', a detail that would have really escalated things should the neighbours have ever found out they were banging.

Now, this might be the point where anyone else would have gone, 'Well, we had a good run, but I guess no more shagging for me,' or, at least, 'Maybe we'll shag outdoors!' But for Dolly and Otto, that just wasn't kinky/ludicrous enough. Dolly asked Otto to move in with her. Not in an 'I'll tell my husband we're through' kind of way, but in a 'Get in the attic and don't make a fucking sound when he's home' kind of a scenario. Otto moved into the attic, empty but for a bed and a typewriter, and remained there *for five years*. In exchange for abandoning every aspect of normal life, he was allowed to scuttle downstairs during the day to pork Dolly and enjoy the library books she brought him. He would write when he couldn't be heard, and even got stories published in pulp fiction magazines under a pen name. Presumably something like Attic Sexington or Sexingly Atticwise.

Fred, meanwhile, started to think he was going insane, or that the house was haunted, when his cigars kept going missing and he was hearing strange noises coming from the attic. While it may seem silly that his mind jumped so quickly to 'ghosts', I would argue it's more rational than thinking, 'You know, I bet there's a typewriter repairman up there who creeps down during the day to fuck my wife.' Fred decided he'd had enough, and planned to move to Los Angeles, taking Dolly with him. This didn't stop the affair, though, as Dolly merely forced her husband to choose a new place with an attic, then sent Otto to move, ahead of their arrival, into his new, slightly hotter, attic.

Arguments between Dolly and Fred weren't solved by the move. You won't be shocked to hear that when one person in a couple is keeping a live-in sex slave in the roof, their problems run deeper than 'We need a nicer house'. Their fights became violent (this story has at least two assholes) and on one night, Otto, fearing for Dolly's life, rushed down the stairs carrying a gun. Fred only had a few moments to register 'Hey you're that repairman who went missing, thank god you're OK!' before he was shot several times in the chest.

Otto and Dolly put together a flimsy alibi, involving a botched burglary, and Otto hid himself away once more. Dolly inherited her husband's money and used it to buy, you guessed it, a house with a slightly larger attic. With – I really must stress – no reason whatsoever for him to be kept there, Otto moved into his new sex attic, while Dolly dated several new men at the same time.

This was to be her downfall. In 1930, she one day asked one of her boyfriends to dispose of the guns used to kill her husband, and gave another boyfriend – who was also her lawyer – a watch that had supposedly been stolen in the 'burglary'. When she broke up with gun boyfriend, he went to the police to tell them how she had asked him to dispose of a weapon in a tar pit, and she was promptly arrested. During her arrest, she asked her lawyer boyfriend to feed her attic boyfriend, like you would a cat. Otto, so pleased to have someone other than Dolly to talk to for the first time in ten years, forgot that it was bad conversational etiquette to immediately confess to all your crimes.

For their odd situation though, the two suffered zero consequences, as by that point Otto had been in his attic for long enough to run down the statute of limitations on manslaughter. They lived to an old age – though, thankfully, Otto finally moved out of his sex roof.

THE US AND THEIR PLAN TO BOMB THE SHIT OUT OF ... THE US

In the 1950s, the US noticed that nuclear bombs had a bit of a bad reputation, largely on the grounds that they were designed to take millions of humans and turn them into radioactive mush. Rather than thinking, 'Ah yeah, they have a bit of a point here, maybe that's bad,' the federal government decided to do a bit of PR work on behalf of the nightmare weapons that will one day destroy the Earth. Or, as they put it, 'Highlight the peaceful applications of nuclear explosive devices and thereby create a climate of world opinion that is more favourable to weapons development and tests.'[1]

One idea – which they dubbed 'Project Chariot', rather than 'Nuke the shit out of Alaska and hope for the best' – was essentially to nuke the shit out of Alaska and hope for the best. The plan was to take a 2.4 megaton bomb and use it to blow a gigantic hole off Cape Thompson in order to create a harbour. Look, I get that nobody really likes digging, but there are several reasons why making holes using a nuclear bomb is worse. The main problem was that there were thousands of people living where the hole was going to be, or hole-adjacent. The feds very much took the 'Ah, can't they just fucking die?' approach for several years, expecting that locals would just have to put up with the harbour creation, and maybe move if it all turned radioactive.

Locals, when the plans leaked, were not fans of the idea. As one man said at the time: 'I'm pretty sure you don't like to see your home being blasted by some other people who don't live in your place like we live in Point Hope.'[2] Side point, but naming your town 'Point Hope' is just begging for some absolutely dogshit events to happen. You might as well have named it 'Lake Nobody Is Going To Twat Us' or 'Cape Everything Is Going To Be Fine Forever'.

Locals also weren't hugely on board with the government contaminating their fishing water with radioactive materials that could turn their food into mutant food. Native Alaskans applied pressure on the US government to not bomb them, which honestly didn't have much of an effect. However, scientists also started to question whether the nuclear bomb would create the big old crater they thought it would, and whether a tiny hole would be worth contaminating the ocean for decades to come.

Rather than admit that their idea was shite, they put the plan on hiatus. Officially, America still plans to nuke the fuck out of America, they just haven't got around to it yet.

THE MAN WHO TURNED PRISONERS INTO BASEBALL STARS

At the turn of the nineteenth century, justice in the state of Wyoming consisted pretty much of hanging and skinning when the new state penitentiary opened – the first in the whole of the United States. For the first ten years, the place was run in the traditional American way, by which I mean there was quite a lot of indefensible human rights abuses and slavery. For example, the prisoners were given just enough food to not die and were forced to work in the in-house broom factory.

In 1911, a new reformer took over as warden, and things looked up. Felix Alston talked a good game, wanting to rehabilitate the prisoners through education and allow them recreation time outside. This may not sound like much, but a lot of the prisoners hadn't seen daylight for ten years.[1] He even arranged for the prisoners to take part in a baseball game, a fate so boring today, however, that it would still contravene the Geneva Convention. (For non-US folks reading this, I should explain that baseball is basically shit rounders.)

Alston assembled a team from the prisoners, the Wyoming State Penitentiary's All Stars, made up mainly of convicted murderers and rapists. While 'All Stars' may not have been strictly accurate, I guess it's difficult to persuade a printer to make T-shirts with the logo 'All Murderers and Sex Offenders'. The team was so good, he sought permission from the governor, Joseph Carey, to allow them to play local teams. Fortunately, Governor Carey was a gambling man and saw this as less of a rehabilitation effort and more of a chance to make an absolute buttload of cash. He approved of the team, and they began their season against the only team in the state with a worse name than the team of murderers: The Wyoming Supply Company Juniors.

In the first game, the All Stars pummelled the stationery boys. Who knew that a life in prison with nothing to entertain you but exercise and dodging shankings would lead you to be better at reacting to and smacking balls than selling toner? The press caught wind of the games, and covered them with great enthusiasm, delving into the players' backgrounds. Before long, the state and country were invested in the team, and placing large bets on them.

The star player – a man named Joseph Seng, who had killed his mistress's husband – got sympathy from the public, who began to petition for his death sentence to be reduced to a sentence that didn't end in him being dead. Weirdly, it worked, and his execution kept getting put off as the season went on. Rumours began to swirl that the governor might not want to execute the guy who kept hitting home runs for the team he kept putting a shitload of cash on.

The captain – George Saban – began to use these rumours to his advantage, telling the team in quite a yelly manner that if they lost games they might be kept in jail for longer, but if they kept winning they might escape execution like Seng. You may not take team talks seriously, but George Saban was actually a fucking murderer, which probably kept their attention. The team continued their winning streak, possibly finding motivation in not wanting to be hanged from the neck until they were dead, which must have been quite the stakes when playing a stationery supplier in a friendly.

The All Stars ended up winning all their games by a wide margin, but problems soon arose. Fellow prisoners who hadn't made the team weren't keen on the idea that they might get executed for the crime of being shit at baseball, as well as their actual crime, while prisoners like Seng might have their executions commuted. The day after Seng was due to be executed, one inmate even tried to kill him. Outside the prison, people began to believe rumours that the governor was keeping Seng alive because he was good at baseball. While I'm no fan of the death penalty, it wasn't great that they were sending the message that if you were really good at sports, your first murder could be on the house.

In response, Alston removed the baseball programme and replaced it with an educational one. Shortly afterwards, with the governor richer from gambling on the team, Seng was executed. Unfortunately, this practice of executing baseball players did not catch on and the 'sport' continues to this day.

JOHN WATTS AND THOMAS SMYTHE

Every time you take a sip of what is laughably called English breakfast tea, you probably don't pause to think, 'Ah that's lovely – I bet some real cunt was behind this,' but, inevitably, there was, and this is evidenced by looking back to the company that pioneered and then dominated the tea trade.

It's difficult to oversell how cartoonishly evil the East India Company truly was. Set up by John Watts and Thomas Smythe in 1600, the company's ethos was basically to sell its (largely) innocuous products by any means necessary, and failing that, by any means unnecessary. Trading in what (on the surface) looked like harmless products, such as sugar, spices and tea, it was also responsible for unimaginable and systematic human suffering. Like if you found out that the Coco Pops monkey made the individual pops by granting each grain of rice sentience before executing them in front of their rice family.

The company, of course, began to use and transport slaves in the 1620s, a practice it kept up for over two hundred years. Before the 1833 Slavery Abolition Act was passed in the UK, several East India Company officials argued against it, making the company one of the few entities even more evil than the British. The officials claimed that the act was interfering in traditional social structures.[1] Imagine shipping your family members across the world to perform forced labour for zero money for the rest of their miserable lives, simply because it was tradition. 'It's silly, I know, but we do it every year and the kids love it!'

Then, in the eighteenth century, the East India Company was having trouble gaining tea from China, as China needed less of the company's goods (cotton and wool) than we needed a cuppa, making trade somewhat imbalanced. Instead of merely accepting this, as you do when, e.g., a shop declines to sell you a TV because you 'haven't got any money', the East India Company began pumping opium that it had grown in India (impoverishing the labourers who farmed it,[2] of course) into China, in order to get China hooked and willing to trade large amounts of tea for it. This is along the same principle as you attempting to buy the aforementioned TV with no money, then shooting the shop assistant full of heroin for long enough to get them addicted to it, then offering them a baggie for the flatscreen.

Unlike most food and fabric companies today (with the obvious exception of Jaffa Cakes, probably), the East India Company had its own fucking military, but to be fair that's the kind of thing you need when you take control of India against India's will. The company slowly took control of the country from the mid-1750s, with a regime that lasted nearly a century before it faced an 1857 rebellion which it couldn't handle. During the uprising, the company of course was responsible for a large number of massacres, before the rebellion was quashed, and many rebels were executed by cannon – an especially cruel punishment as 1) victims believed that they could not get into the afterlife without a complete body, and 2) they were being executed with a fucking cannon.

Following the rebellion, the company was nationalised by the British Empire, the only entity whose reputation could be improved by incorporating a bloodthirsty version of PG Tips.

JAMES JAMESON

James Jameson – a rare double James – was heir to the Irish Jameson whiskey fortune, and the great-great-grandson of its creator John Jameson. With the money he was set to inherit from his grandad, James would have lived a life of luxury and ease. All he had to do was sit back, relax and try not to pay witness to some cannibalism. An easy task, you might think, but not so for James Jameson.

James joined a tour of Ribakiba in the Congo in the 1880s, led by explorer Henry Morton Stanley. The trip was marketed as a relief mission to rescue Emin Pasha (the governor of the Egyptian province of Equatoria who was believed to be in danger), but the trip had a second purpose, which was to annex more land for the Belgian empire. While on the expedition, Jameson came across a local slave trader who went by the name of Tippu Tip.[1] While in conversation with the slaver, the topic shifted towards cannibalism. I'll hazard a guess that you can go years, or even decades without pivoting conversation in that direction, and would take extra care not to if you were in the presence of actual cannibals. However, that's the way the conversation went (maybe they ran out of weather chat), and Tip relayed an anecdote about how after a battle, the locals had killed and eaten many of their enemies, washing the human meat in a well before eating it. When he drank the water the next day, he found it oily and yellow from human fat.

Here's where things get a little complicated, as this next part of the story has several versions depending on who was asked.

In Jameson's version, he claims that during his conversation with Tip, he told him that back home nobody believed the stories of cannibalism were real. Tip then said to Jameson, 'Give me a bit of cloth and see.' Jameson, according to his own account, immediately sent his boy for six handkerchiefs to give to Tip – rather than, for example, simply not calling the bluff of a slave trader who had recently told an anecdote about drinking from a well of human fat.

Jameson later wrote that he believed it all to be a joke, but upon Tip receiving the handkerchiefs, a slave girl of about ten was killed right there and then in front of them, before being butchered and washed as though they were preparing meat. Naturally, Jameson then went home and 'made some small sketches of the scene while still fresh in [his] memory'.[2] He then hung around shooting the shit with Tippu Tip for the duration of the visit, never once asking, 'What the fuck?'

However, according to Assad Farran, a Sudanese translator on the expedition, Jameson was much more involved than simply believing he was playing along with a 'hilarious' cannibalism jape. Farran gave an affidavit to the *New York Times* claiming that Jameson had expressed his curiosity to see cannibalism, and had then purchased the slave girl using the handkerchiefs. While Jameson watched, she was taken to the chiefs of the tribe and presented as a gift, before being butchered and eaten. 'Jameson in the meantime was making rough sketches of the horrible scene. Then he went to his camp, where he finished the sketches as watercolours' – the affidavit stated – which he then proudly showed around the other officers.

Jameson died in 1888, still denying that he knew what was going to happen to the girl, but it probably didn't help his credibility that he had gone on a trip that was on behalf of *King Leopold the fucking II* (for the uninitiated, see page 109), before making detailed sketches of the gruesome act to show off to all his buddies.

DUON H. MILLER

As this is the end of the book, I thought I'd pick a nice big asshole to end on. While not necessarily the biggest of the assholes included in this book, Duon H. Miller is certainly one of the most irritating, and he is also an excellent example of how history repeats itself. During the Covid pandemic it has been hard to move for cranks claiming that the disease doesn't exist, is 'just flu' or that the vaccines are some sort of plot by Bill Gates to microchip everyone, a plan so rumblable you could even find it using Bing.

This sort of pandemic denial is by no means new. Hell, there were probably people during the Black Death claiming 'Ring-a-ring-a-roses' was government propaganda designed to stop the freedoms of serfs to die drowning in their own pus, AS IS THEIR CHOICE. One pandemic-denier – the aforementioned Miller – is notable for attempting to discredit the polio vaccine, just as it began to save millions of lives.

Polio is an especially nasty disease, causing everything from meningitis to paralysis in severe cases. It was rife in the early 1950s, when American virologist Jonas Salk discovered a potential vaccine for polio in 1952 and immediately volunteered himself and his entire family as test subjects (as part of a human trial). All of them developed antibodies for the disease, and Salk went on to catapult himself into legendary good-guy status by refusing to patent the vaccine, explaining that it belonged to the people: 'There is no patent. Could you patent the Sun?'

His Wario, meanwhile, began spreading the rumour that the vaccine itself was dangerous, and that the virus that caused polio didn't really exist. Duon H. Miller was a cosmetics manufacturer, famous for his 'Vita-fluff' shampoo. Fancying a crack at something which wasn't nourishing people's roots, he campaigned against the vaccines and the potential treatment gamma globulin[1] on the (racist) grounds that it 'can cause Negro, Japanese or other racial characteristics to show up in the second or third generation of persons who take it, if it comes from the blood of such persons of such races'.[2] During a postal campaign Miller sent out leaflets proclaiming 'Fake Polio Vaccine May Kill Your Child!',[3] which, to be fair, if you go on word count, is 5/7ths correct. The most bizarre part was that he firmly believed that polio – which saw regular outbreaks, as you might expect of a virus – was caused by overconsumption of sugary drinks depleting people's calcium, as if a new massive caseload in e.g. New York was caused by a sudden increase of everybody necking Sprite. This is especially stupid given that polio has likely been around since the time of the ancient Egyptians.[4] Miller probably believed 'Maybe Tutankhamun wouldn't have died if he'd just laid off the Irn-Bru.'

While overconsuming sugary drinks is by no means great (side note: please don't throw this in my face if I launch a line of Feltonade) it obviously wasn't causing polio. Miller nonetheless continued to push the line that it was, and that 'thousands of little white coffins will be used to bury victims of Salk's heinous and fraudulent vaccine'.[5]

Before long, the shampoo magnate was fined $1,000 for sending libellous material through the mail, forcing him to ~~rethink his actions~~ use a different mail carrier, before he was eventually ordered by the court to 'keep his nose out of polio' (with slightly more legalistic wording).

Fortunately for the world, Miller's opinions were largely ignored due to the fact that – upon vaccination – everyone suddenly stopped getting polio, despite regularly chugging away on Coca-Cola like diabetes didn't exist.

ACKNOWLEDGEMENTS

My thanks to everyone at Little, Brown – from design to production – for getting the book off the ground, and to Emanuel Santos for the perfect illustrations. You are, as ever, all extremely talented people. Special thanks to Emily Barrett for the chance to write about my speciality subject: terrible people doing awful things for no good reason. And to Sarah Kennedy for her excellent edits and suggestions, which improved the book no end.

And of course, thank you to all the godawful assholes from history for being dicks. You are the real MVPs.

NOTES

DOMITIAN

1 Gaius Suetonius Tranquillus, 'Suetonius: Life of Domitian', *The Lives of the Caesars* <http://penelope.uchicago.edu/Thayer/E/Roman/Texts/Suetonius/12Caesars/Domitian*.html> [accessed 15 May 2022].
2 Ibid.
3 Joseph Castro, 'Who Invented the Mirror?', Live Science, 2013 <https://www.livescience.com/34466-who-invented-mirror.html> [accessed 15 May 2022].
4 Suetonius.
5 Cassius Dio, 'Epitome of Book 67', *Roman History by Cassius Dio* <http://penelope.uchicago.edu/Thayer/e/roman/texts/cassius_dio/67*.html> [accessed 25 May 2022].

THE DOCTOR WHO LIKED TO MAKE BABIES CRY

1 John B. Watson and Rosalie Rayner, 'Conditioned Emotional Reactions', *Journal of Experimental Psychology* 3(1), 1–14 <https://psychclassics.yorku.ca/Watson/emotion.htm> [accessed 31 March 2022].
2 Ibid.
3 Ibid.
4 Ibid.

EMPEROR QIN SHI HUANG

1 Carrie Gracie, 'Qin Shi Huang: The Ruthless Emperor Who Burned Books', BBC News, 2012 <https://www.bbc.com/news/magazine-19922863> [accessed 13 April 2022].
2 Wu Hung, *The Wu Liang Shrine: The Ideology of Early Chinese Pictorial Art* (Stanford: Stanford University Press, 1989).
3 'Burning the Books and Killing the Scholars: Representing the Atrocities of the First Emperor of China', US-China Institute <https://china.usc.edu/calendar/burning-books-and-killing-scholars-representing-atrocities-first-emperor-china> [accessed 13 April 2022].
4 'The Emperor with an Ego Big Enough for All Time', *Sunday Times*, 2007 <https://www.thetimes.co.uk/article/the-emperor-with-an-ego-big-enough-for-all-time-65xkpms9mb6> [accessed 13 April 2022].

QUEEN RANAVALONA I

1 Gwyn Campbell, 'The State and Pre-Colonial Demographic History: The Case of Nineteenth-Century Madagascar', *The Journal of African History*, 32.3 (1991), 415–45 <https://doi.org/10.1017/S0021853700031534>.

THE EXECUTIONER WHO WAS NOTORIOUSLY BAD AT EXECUTIONS

1 'The Gruesome Reason Why Newgate Prison Used To Be Known As 'Jack Ketch's Kitchen', Londonist, 2018 <https://londonist.com/london/history/jack-ketch-dodgy-axeman> [accessed 31 March 2022].
2 Juré Fiorillo, *Great Bastards of History: True and Riveting Accounts of the Most Famous Illegitimate Children Who Went on to Achieve Greatness* (Beverly, MA: Fair Winds Press, 2013).
3 'The Execution of the Duke of Monmouth', *Port Folio*, 1826, 97–99.

THE DOCTOR WHO TRIED TO MAKE A HUMANZEE

1 Jerry Bergman, 'Human-Ape Hybridization: A Failed Attempt to Prove Darwinism', Institute of Creation Research, 2009 <https://www.icr.org/article/human-ape-hybridization-failed-attempt/> [accessed 31 March 2022].
2 Stephanie Pain, 'Blasts from the Past: The Soviet Ape-Man Scandal', *New Scientist*, 2008 <https://www.newscientist.com/article/mg19926701-000-blasts-from-the-past-the-soviet-ape-man-scandal/> [accessed 31 March 2022].
3 Kirill Rossiianov, 'Beyond Species: Il'ya Ivanov and His Experiments on Cross-Breeding Humans with Anthropoid Apes', *Science in Context*, 15.2 (2011) <https://doi.org/10.1017/S0269889702000455>.

CHRISTOPHER COLUMBUS

1 'Columbus' <https://www2.latech.edu/~bmagee/212/columbus/columbus_notes.htm> [accessed 13 April 2022].
2 Dan MacGuill, 'Did Christopher Columbus Seize, Sell, and Export Sex Slaves?', Snopes.com, 2018 <https://www.snopes.com/fact-check/columbus-sex-slaves/> [accessed 14 April 2022].
3 Dylan Matthews, '9 Reasons Christopher Columbus Was a Murderer, Tyrant, and Scoundrel', Vox, 2015 <https://www.vox.com/2014/10/13/6957875/christopher-columbus-murderer-tyrant-scoundrel> [accessed 14 April 2022].
4 George E. Tinker and Mark Freeland, 'Thief, Slave Trader, Murderer: Christopher Columbus and Caribbean Population Decline', *Wicazo Sa Review*, 23.1 (2008), 25–50 <https://doi.org/10.1353/wic.2008.0002>.
5 Kris Lane, 'Five Myths about Christopher Columbus', *Washington Post*, 2015, <https://www.washingtonpost.com/opinions/five-myths-about-christopher-columbus/2015/10/08/3e80f358-6d23-11e5-b31c-d80d62b53e28_story.html> [accessed 13 April 2022].
6 History com Editors, 'Why Columbus Day Courts Controversy', HISTORY <https://www.history.com/news/columbus-day-controversy> [accessed 13 April 2022].

THE MAN WHO GOT THREE JESUSES AND MADE THEM FIGHT

1 Milton Rokeach, *The Three Christs of Ypsilanti* (New York: New York Review Books, 2011).
2 Ibid.

PETER THE GREAT

1 'Catherine I (1684–1727)', Encyclopedia.com <https://www.encyclopedia.com/women/encyclopedias-almanacs-transcripts-and-maps/catherine-i-1684-1727> [accessed 15 May 2022].
2 Natasha Frost, 'What Happened to the Severed Head of Peter the Great's Wife's Lover', Atlas Obscura, 2017 <http://www.atlasobscura.com/articles/kunstkamera-museum-head-jar-peter-great-lover-wife> [accessed 15 May 2022].

THE EGG SMASHERS OF SAN FRANCISCO

1 Jessica Gingrich, 'When California Went to War Over Eggs', *Smithsonian Magazine*, 2019 <https://www.smithsonianmag.com/history/when-california-went-war-over-eggs-180971960/> [accessed 31 March 2022].
2 Ibid.

THE VARIED ABUSERS OF OOFTY GOOFTY

1 Katie Dowd, 'One of SF's First Celebs Was a Man You Paid to Beat with a Baseball Bat', SFGATE, 2021 <https://www.sfgate.com/sfhistory/article/2021-04-oofty-goofty-sf-eccentrics-sideshow-16121362.php> [accessed 31 March 2022].
2 McMihail, 'History Teaches Us: Things We Do For Entertainment', 2017 <https://web.archive.org/web/20210124051014/https://thequotes.com/blog/history-teaches-us-things-entertainment> [accessed 31 March 2022].

SAINT OLGA OF KIEV

1 'Korosten (Iskorosten): Small Town with a Great History', Korosten City, 2009 <https://web.archive.org/web/20091026051916/http://geocities.com/korostencity/iskorosten.htm> [accessed 31 March 2022].
2 Dana Rovang, 'Olga of Kyiv: Ingenious Avenger, Leader, and Saint', Obscure Histories, 2022 <https://www.obscurehistories.com/post/olga-of-kyiv-ingenious-avenger-leader-and-saint> [accessed 24 April 2022].

IVAN THE TERRIBLE

1 Jaclyn Anglis, 'Why Russian Tyrant Ivan The Terrible Was Even More Brutal Than His Name Suggests', All That's Interesting, 2021 <https://allthatsinteresting.com/ivan-the-terrible> [accessed 13 April 2022].
2 Ibid.
3 Viacheslav Olegovich Shpakovskiĭ and David Nicolle, *Armies of Ivan the Terrible: Russian Troops 1505–1700* (Oxford; New York: Osprey, 2006).
4 'Novgorod Massacre: Ivan The Terrible Orders A Massacre In Novgorod', HistoryCollection.com, 2017 <https://historycollection.com/day-history-ivan-terrible-orders-massacre-novgorod-1570/> [accessed 13 April 2022].
5 Ibid.
6 Anglis.

THE BEAR TRAINER WHO WASN'T TOO FUSSED IF YOU WERE OR WEREN'T A BEAR

1 Shane Daly, 'The Bear from Waterford – West Cork People', *West Cork People*, 2020 <https://westcorkpeople.ie/columnists/the-bear-from-waterford/> [accessed 31 March 2022].
2 Michael Cronin, 'What Have the French Ever Done for Us?', *Irish Times*, 2018 <https://www.irishtimes.com/culture/books/what-have-the-french-ever-done-for-us-1.3553807> [accessed 31 March 2022].

THE MAN WHO KILLED SANTA IN FRONT OF EVERYBODY

1 'Editor Killed Santa', *Tucson Daily Citizen*, 1958.
2 Johanna Eubank, 'The Man Who Killed Santa Claus', Tucson.com, 2021 <https://tucson.com/morguetales/the-man-who-killed-santa-claus/article_713907ba-ca4e-11e7-8efc-5b9847004e22.html> [accessed 31 March 2022].

THE PRANKSTER WHO COULD HAVE
CAUSED A NUCLEAR MELTDOWN

1 Carol Nichol, 'That Time Scientists Ran Experiments on Whether Pinching Someone in the Butt Could Cause a Nuclear Meltdown', Today I Found Out, 2020 <http://www.todayifoundout.com/index.php/2020/10/that-time-scientists-ran-experiments-on-whether-pinching-someone-in-the-butt-could-cause-a-nuclear-meltdown/> [accessed 31 March 2022].
2 William McKeown, *Idaho Falls: The Untold Story of America's First Nuclear Accident* (Toronto: ECW Press, 2013).

COMMODUS

1 Cassius Dio, 'Epitome of Book 73', *Roman History by Cassius Dio* <https://penelope.uchicago.edu/Thayer/E/Roman/Texts/Cassius_Dio/73*.html> [accessed 13 April 2022].
2 Ibid.
3 Dave Roos, 'The True History of Commodus, the Mad Emperor of Ancient Rome', HowStuffWorks, 2021 <https://history.howstuffworks.com/historical-figures/commodus.htm> [accessed 13 April 2022].

THE DOCTOR WHO THOUGHT GOAT
BALLS COULD CURE EVERYTHING

1 R. Alton Lee, *The Bizarre Careers of John R. Brinkley* (Lexington: University of Kentucky, 2002).
2 Mike Vago, 'This medical fraud's miracle cure involved implanting goat testicles into humans', AV Club, 2020, <https://www.avclub.com/this-medical-fraud-s-miracale-cure-involved-transplantin-1843720760> [accessed 31 March 2022].
3 Frank Wardlaw, 'The Goat-Gland Man', *Southwest Review*, 66 (1981), 203–9.

ELIZABETH BÁTHORY/ELIZABETH BÁTHORY'S ACCUSERS,
DEPENDING ON YOUR PERSPECTIVE

1 John Kuroski, 'Did Elizabeth Báthory, The "Blood Countess," Actually Deserve Her Nickname?', All That's Interesting, 2021 <https://allthatsinteresting.com/elizabeth-bathory> [accessed 3 April 2022].
2 Léonie Chao-Fong, 'The Blood Countess: 10 Facts About Elizabeth Báthory', History Hit, 2021 <https://www.historyhit.com/the-blood-countess-facts-about-elizabeth-bathory/> [accessed 3 April 2022].
3 Kathryn Whitbourne and Josh Clark, 'Was Countess Elizabeth Bathory the World's Most Prolific Serial Killer?', HowStuffWorks <https://history.howstuffworks.com/history-vs-myth/hungarian-countess-serial-killer.htm> [accessed 3 April 2022].
4 Dr Irma Szádeczky-Kardoss, 'The Bloody Countess? An Examination of the Life and Trial of Erzsébet Báthory', *Notes on Hungarian History*, 2014 <https://notesonhungary.wordpress.com/2014/05/31/the-bloody-countess/> [accessed 3 April 2022].

THE FIRST PEOPLE TO CONDUCT BIOLOGICAL WARFARE

1 Natasha Ishak, 'Was The Black Death Started By An Act Of Biological Warfare?', All That's Interesting, 2020 <https://allthatsinteresting.com/when-did-the-black-plague-start> [accessed 3 April 2022].
2 Mark Wheelis, 'Biological Warfare at the 1346 Siege of Caffa', *Emerging Infectious Diseases*, 8.9 (2002), 971–75 <https://doi.org/10.3201/eid0809.010536>.

JAMES 'DR SHITS' MORRISON

1 David Bingham, 'The London Dead: The Pills That Cured All Ills; James Morison the Hygeist (1770–-1840), Kensal Green Cemetery', The London Dead, 2014 <http://thelondondead.blogspot.com/2014/11/the-pills-that-cure-all-ills-james.html>.
2 James Morrison, 'Morisoniana, Or, Family Adviser of the British College of Health: Being a Collection of the Works of Mr Morison, the Hygeist … Forming a Complete Manual for Individuals and Families, for Every Thing That Regards Preserving Them in Health and Curing Their Diseases … With an Appendix, Containing a Short Treatise on … Small Pox', Wellcome Collection <https://wellcomecollection.org/works/hf8m8y8a> [accessed 31 March 2022].
3 'Morrison and Another v Harmer and Another', vLex <https://vlex.co.uk/vid/morrison-and-another-v-802857181> [accessed 31 March 2022].
4 'Medical Miscellany', *Boston Medical and Surgical Journal*, 10–11 (1834), 180–81.
5 Marc Kuroski, 'Meet James Morison, The 19th-Century Quack Doctor Who Tried To Cure Everything With Laxatives', All That's Interesting, 2021 <https://allthatsinteresting.com/james-morison> [accessed 31 March 2022].
6 'Morrison and Another v Harmer and Another'.

CLEVER HANS THE HORSE

1 Laasya Samhita and Hans J. Gross, 'The "Clever Hans Phenomenon" Revisited', *Communicative & Integrative Biology*, 6.6 (2013) <https://doi.org/10.4161/cib.27122>.

VICTORIANO ÁLVAREZ

1 Marissa Brook, 'The Tyrant of Clipperton Island', Damn Interesting, 2012 <https://www.damninteresting.com/the-tyrant-of-clipperton-island/> [accessed 3 April 2022].
2 Inma Gil Rosendo, 'La Desconocida Y Trágica Historia de Clipperton, El Último Territorio Que Perdió México', BBC News Mundo, 2021 <https://www.bbc.com/mundo/noticias-america-latina-55681035> [accessed 3 April 2022].

KING EDWARD III

1 'The Statute of Laborers; 1351', The Avalon Project – documents in law, history and diplomacy, 1998 <https://avalon.law.yale.edu/medieval/statlab.asp> [accessed 3 April 2022].
2 Ibid.

THE US AND THEIR RIDICULOUS PLAN TO NUKE THE MOON

1 J. Reiffel, 'A Study of Lunar Research Flights', Armour Research Foundation, 1 (1959) <https://web.archive.org/web/20190407000018/https://nsarchive2.gwu.edu/NSAEBB/NSAEBB479/docs/EBB-Moon02.pdf> [accessed 31 March 2022].
2 Antony Barnett, 'US planned one big nuclear blast for mankind', *Observer*, 2000, <https://www.theguardian.com/science/2000/may/14/spaceexploration.theobserver> [accessed 30 May 2022].

HERMAN SÖRGEL

1 Toon Lambrechts, 'The Bonkers Real-Life Plan to Drain the Mediterranean and Merge Africa and Europe', Atlas Obscura, 2016 <http://www.atlasobscura.com/articles/the-bonkers-reallife-plan-to-drain-the-mediterranean-and-merge-africa-and-europe> [accessed 31 March 2022].

2 Ricarda Vidal, 'Atlantropa: The Colossal 1920s Plan to Dam the Mediterranean and Create a Supercontinent', The Conversation, 2015 <https://web.archive.org/web/20210214224234/https://theconversation.com/atlantropa-the-colossal-1920s-plan-to-dam-the-mediterranean-and-create-a-supercontinent-47370> [accessed 31 March 2022].
3 Frank Jacobs, 'Damming the Mediterranean: The Atlantropa Project', Big Think, 2010 <https://web.archive.org/web/20210216210125/https://bigthink.com/strange-maps/287-dam-you-mediterranean-the-atlantropa-project/> [accessed 31 March 2022].

HANNAH DUSTON AND THE SCALP-HUNGRY COLONISERS

1 Barbara Cutter, 'The Gruesome Story of Hannah Duston, Whose Slaying of Indians Made Her an American Folk "Hero"', Smithsonian Magazine, 2018 <https://www.smithsonianmag.com/history/gruesome-story-hannah-duston-american-colonist-whose-slaying-indians-made-her-folk-hero-180968721/> [accessed 15 May 2022].
2 Diane E. Foulds, 'Who Scalped Whom? – Historians Suggest Indians Were As Much Victims As Perpetrators', Hawthorne in Salem <http://www.hawthorneinsalem.org/ScholarsForum/MMD2263.html> [accessed 15 May 2022].
3 Ibid.
4 Cecil Adams, 'Did Native Americans Learn Scalping from Europeans?', The Straight Dope, 2006 <https://www.straightdope.com/21343807/did-native-americans-learn-scalping-from-europeans> [accessed 15 May 2022].

THE GREEK MYSTIC WITH AN IMPRESSIVE COMMAND OF SOCK PUPPETS

1 Lucian (trans. H. W. Fowler and F. G. Fowler), 'Alexander the Oracle-Monger', <https://monadnock.net/lucian/alexander.html> [accessed 25 May 2022].
2 Ibid.
3 Ibid.
4 Ibid.

THE SEX CULT THAT TRIED TO TAKE OVER OREGON

1 Sam Wollaston, 'Growing up in the Wild Wild Country Cult: "You Heard People Having Sex All the Time, like Baboons"', Guardian, 2018 <http://www.theguardian.com/tv-and-radio/2018/apr/24/wild-wild-country-netflix-cult-sex-noa-maxwell-bhagwan-shree-rajneesh-commune-childhood> [accessed 31 March 2022].
2 Gilles Messier, 'That Time an Oregon Free-Love Cult Launched the Largest Bioterror Attack in US History', Today I Found Out, 2021 <http://www.todayifoundout.com/index.php/2021/07/that-time-an-oregon-free-love-cult-launched-the-largest-bioterror-attack-in-us-history/> [accessed 31 March 2022].
3 Les Zaitz, '25 Years after Rajneeshee Commune Collapsed, Truth Spills out – Part 1 of 5', The Oregonian, 2019 <https://web.archive.org/web/20220107134623/https://www.oregonlive.com/rajneesh/2011/04/part_one_it_was_worse_than_we.html> [accessed 31 March 2022].
4 'The City Council, Whose Members Are Followers of Indian . . .', UPI, 1984 <https://www.upi.com/Archives/1984/03/08/The-City-Council-whose-members-are-followers-of-Indian/8091447570000/> [accessed 31 March 2022].

SIR BASIL ZAHAROFF

1 Smithsonian Magazine and Mike Dash, 'The Mysterious Mr Zedzed: The Wickedest Man in the World', Smithsonian Magazine, 2012 <https://www.smithsonianmag.com/history/the-mysterious-mr-zedzed-the-wickedest-man-in-the-world-97435790/> [accessed 3 April 2022].

2 Jonathan Grant, '"Merchants of Death": The International Traffic in Arms', Origins <https://origins.osu.edu/article/merchants-death-international-traffic-arms> [accessed 3 April 2022].

THE MAN WHO PRETENDED HE HADN'T JUST LOST
A LION IN BIRMINGHAM CITY CENTRE

1 Frank Charles Bostock, *The Training of Wild Animals*, ed. Ellen Velvin (New York: Century, 1903).
2 Bethan Bell, 'When a Lion Prowled the Streets of Birmingham', BBC News, 2017 <https://www.bbc.com/news/uk-england-39799098> [accessed 31 March 2022].

OLIVER CROMWELL

1 Frances Mulraney, 'Oliver Cromwell's War Crimes, Massacre of Drogheda in 1649', Irish Central, 2022 <https://www.irishcentral.com/roots/history/oliver-cromwells-massacre-of-drogheda-1649> [accessed 15 May 2022].
2 Oliver Cromwell and Thomas Carlyle, *Oliver Cromwell's Letters and Speeches, Volume 1* (Chestnut Hill, MA: Elibron Classics, 2005).

JEANNE DE CLISSON

1 M. A. Delaney, 'Jeanne de Clisson: The Lioness of Brittany', History of Yesterday, 2021 <https://historyofyesterday.com/jeanne-de-clisson-the-lioness-of-brittany-95288b20b597> [accessed 3 April 2022].
2 Julia Métraux, 'The Pirate Queen Who Avenged Her Husband's Death on the High Seas', Narratively, 2021 <https://narratively.com/the-pirate-queen-who-avenged-her-husbands-death-on-the-high-seas/> [accessed 3 April 2022].

EMPEROR ZHENGDE

1 Elizabeth Lundin, 'History's Nutcases: The Zhengde Emperor', History Things, 2021 <https://historythings.com/historys-nutcases-the-zhengde-emperor/> [accessed 3 April 2022].
2 *Writing Women in Late Imperial China*, ed. Ellen Widmer and Kang-i Sun Chang (Stanford: Stanford University Press, 1997).

THE REPUBLICAN WHO ESSENTIALLY MADE HIMSELF KING

1 'Robespierre: His Life, Death & Bloody Deeds In The French Revolution', History Extra, 2021 <https://www.historyextra.com/period/modern/robespierre-man-of-terror/> [accessed 13 April 2022].
2 Callum McKelvie, 'What Was the Reign of Terror?', Live Science, 2021 <https://www.livescience.com/reign-of-terror.html> [accessed 13 April 2022].
3 'The Law of 22 Prairial Year II (10 June 1794)', *John Hall Stewart, A Documentary History of the French Revolution* (New York: Macmillan, 1951), 528–31, 1794 <https://revolution.chnm.org/d/439> [accessed 13 April 2022].
4 'Maximilien Robespierre: On the Principles of Political Morality, February 1794', Fordham University Modern History Sourcebook, <https://sourcebooks.fordham.edu/mod/1794robespierre.asp> [accessed 5 June 2022].
5 'Reign of Terror', Britannica <https://www.britannica.com/event/Reign-of-Terror> [accessed 13 April 2022].

CARAVAGGIO

1 'Respected Historical Figures Who Were Actually Terrible People', Grunge, 2021 <https://www.grunge.com/69542/respected-historical-figures-actually-terrible-people/> [accessed 31 March 2022].
2 Eva Sarah Molcard, '21 Facts About Caravaggio', Sothebys.com, 2019 <https://www.sothebys.com/en/articles/21-facts-about-caravaggio> [accessed 31 March 2022].

CHARLES X

1 'Haiti: A Brief History of a Complex Nation', Institute of Haitian Studies <https://web.archive.org/web/20180515015407/https://haitianstudies.ku.edu/haiti-history> [accessed 14 April 2022].
2 John Henley, 'Haiti: A Long Descent to Hell', *Guardian*, 2010 <https://www.theguardian.com/world/2010/jan/14/haiti-history-earthquake-disaster> [accessed 14 April 2022].
3 Choi Hyeyoon (Alyssa), 'How Colonial-Era Debt Helped Shape Haiti's Poverty and Political Unrest', ABC News, 2021 <https://abcnews.go.com/US/colonial-era-debt-helped-shape-haitis-poverty-political/story?id=78851735> [accessed 14 April 2022].
4 Henley, quoting the historian Alex von Tunzelmann.

THE WORLD'S BIGGEST MISER

1 Kat Eschner, 'The Peculiar Story of the Witch of Wall Street', *Smithsonian Magazine*, 2017 <https://www.smithsonianmag.com/smart-news/peculiar-story-hetty-green-aka-witch-wall-street-180967258/> [accessed 31 March 2022].
2 Therese Oneill, 'The Life and Times of Hetty the Hoarder, the Witch of Wall Street', Mental Floss, 2013 <https://www.mentalfloss.com/article/49379/life-and-times-hetty-hoarder-witch-wall-street> [accessed 31 March 2022].

THE CIA AGENTS TURNED PRANKSTERS

1 Jordan Clark, 'PSYWAR in the Philippines | ASWANG of the CIA', The Aswang Project, 2015 <https://www.aswangproject.com/psywar-philippines-aswang-cia/> [accessed 31 March 2022].
2 Ibid.
3 Ibid.
4 Anri Ichimura, 'How the CIA Used the Aswang to Win a War in the Philippines', Esquiremag.ph, 2019 <https://www.esquiremag.ph/long-reads/features/cia-aswang-war-a00304-a2416-20191019-lfrm> [accessed 31 March 2022].

THE STRAW HAT RIOTERS

1 'Straw Hat Smashing Orgy Bares Heads from Battery to Bronx', *New York Tribune*, 1922 <https://chroniclingamerica.loc.gov/lccn/sn83030214/1922-09-16/ed-1/seq-3/> [accessed 31 March 2022].
2 'City Has Wild Night of Straw Hat Riots', *New York Times*, 1922 <https://timesmachine.nytimes.com/timesmachine/1922/09/16/99070942.pdf> [accessed 31 March 2022].

THE FRUIT COMPANY THAT PUT BANANAS BEFORE WORKERS' RIGHTS

1 Eugene Baraka, Mary S. Willis and Brice A. Ishimwe, 'What Kigali's Open-Air Markets Reveal about Achieving Food and Nutrition Security: The Role of African Indigenous Crops', *Agriculture & Food Security*, 11.1 (2022) <https://doi.org/10.1186/s40066-022-00359-4>.

2 Daniel Kurtz-Phelan, 'Bananas: How the United Fruit Company Shaped the World – Peter Chapman, Book Review', *New York Times*, 2008 <https://www.nytimes.com/2008/03/02/books/review/Kurtz-Phelan-t.html> [accessed 3 April 2022].

3 Ibid.

4 Mark Oliver, 'The Banana Wars: How The US Plundered Central America On Behalf Of Corporations', All That's Interesting, 2017 <https://allthatsinteresting.com/banana-wars> [accessed 3 April 2022].

ACTION PARK

1 'The Shocking True Story of America's Deadliest Theme Park', *New Zealand Herald*, 2019 <https://web.archive.org/web/20201127121818/www.nzherald.co.nz/travel/the-shocking-true-story-of-americas-deadliest-theme-park/MPAMM6YYTFFYG4MPYUXKN2I5E4/> [accessed 31 March 2022].

LEOPOLD II OF BELGIUM

1 Peter Preskar, 'Leopold II and The Hidden Holocaust', Medium, 2020 <https://historyofyesterday.com/leopold-ii-9c0277a26710> [accessed 15 May 2022].

THOMAS MIDGLEY JR

1 Joseph A. Williams, 'This 1920s Inventor Sped Up Climate Change With His Chemical Creations', HISTORY, 2019 <https://www.history.com/news/cfcs-leaded-gasoline-inventions-thomas-midgley> [accessed 31 March 2022].

2 Aslihan Babayigit, Hans-Gerd Boyen, and Bert Conings, 'Environment versus Sustainable Energy: The Case of Lead Halide Perovskite-Based Solar Cells', *MRS Energy & Sustainability*, 5.1 (2018), 15 <https://doi.org/10.1557/mre.2017.17>.

3 Deborah Blum, 'Looney Gas and Lead Poisoning: A Short, Sad History', *Wired*, 2013 <https://web.archive.org/web/20150507065440/https://www.wired.com/2013/01/looney-gas-and-lead-poisoning-a-short-sad-history/> [accessed 31 March 2022].

4 Susan Fourtané, 'Thomas Midgley Jr: The Man Who Harmed the World the Most', 2018 <https://interestingengineering.com/thomas-midgley-jr-the-man-who-harmed-the-world-the-most> [accessed 3 April 2022].

THE WOMAN WHO KEPT HER LOVERS IN THE ATTIC

1 Erin Kelly, 'The Married Woman Who Kept Her Lover In The Attic', All That's Interesting, 2017 <https://allthatsinteresting.com/dolly-oesterreich> [accessed 31 March 2022].

2 Cecilia Rasmussen, '"Bat Man" Case: A Lurid Tale of Love and Death', *LA Times*, 1995 <https://web.archive.org/web/20170330030135/http://articles.latimes.com/1995-03-20/local/me-44878_1_dolly-oesterreich> [accessed 31 March 2022].

THE US AND THEIR PLAN TO BOMB THE SHIT OUT OF ... THE US

1 'From the Archives: Morey Wolfson', University Libraries, 2018 <https://www.colorado.edu/libraries/2018/06/02/archives-morey-wolfson> [accessed 15 May 2022].

2 Dan O'Neill, *The Firecracker Boys: H-Bombs, Inupiat Eskimos and the Roots of the Environmental Movement* (New York: Basic Books, 2007).

THE MAN WHO TURNED PRISONERS INTO BASEBALL STARS

1 Shannon Quinn, 'In 1910, Death Row Inmates Played Baseball For Their Lives', History Collection, 2019 <https://web.archive.org/web/20220220220228/https://historycollection.com/in-1910-death-row-inmates-played-baseball-for-their-lives/> [accessed 31 March 2022].

JOHN WATTS AND THOMAS SMYTHE

1 Nancy Gardner Cassels, *Social Legislation of the East India Company: Public Justice Versus Public Instruction* (New Delhi: SAGE India, 2010) <http://www.SLQ.eblib.com.au/patron/FullRecord.aspx?p=669124> [accessed 3 April 2022].
2 Soutik Biswas, 'How Britain's Opium Trade Impoverished Indians', BBC News, 2019 <https://www.bbc.com/news/world-asia-india-49404024> [accessed 3 April 2022].

JAMES JAMESON

1 John Kuroski, 'This Jameson Whiskey Heir Once Bought A Girl Just To Watch Her Be Eaten By Cannibals', All That's Interesting, 2017 <https://allthatsinteresting.com/james-jameson-cannibal> [accessed 31 March 2022].
2 James S. Jameson, *The Story of the Rear Column of the Emin Pasha Relief Expedition* (New York: Negro Universities Press, 1969).

DUON H. MILLER

1 Stephen E. Mawdsley, 'The Clinical Trials on Gamma Globulin for Polio: Victims of Marketing Success', *Canadian Medical Association Journal*, 189.29 (2017), E967–69 <https://doi.org/10.1503/cmaj.170232>.
2 Nick Keppler, 'One Lonely, Wealthy Man's Crusade Against the Polio Vaccine', Slate Magazine, 2021 <https://slate.com/news-and-politics/2021/11/polio-vaccine-antivaxxer-history-duon-miller.html> [accessed 3 April 2022].
3 'Foe of Polio Vaccine Faces Libel Charges', *Miami Herald*, 1954.
4 CDC, 'What Is Polio?', Centers for Disease Control and Prevention, 2021 <https://www.cdc.gov/polio/what-is-polio/index.htm> [accessed 3 April 2022].
5 'Foe of Polio Vaccine Faces Libel Charges'.